This Text Book is useful for Sir Parshurambhau College, Pune and other Universities as well as Competitive Exams.

Business Economics - I (Micro)

F.Y.B.Com. (Sem. - I)

Sachin Kamble
(M.A., NET.)
S. P. College, Pune.

Payal Pawar
(M.Sc., SET.)
S. P. College, Pune.

2019

Price: 100/-

SUCCESS PUBLICATIONS

Published by
Dr. Rajesh M. Patne
Success Publications
Radha Krishna Apartment, 535, Shaniwar Peth,
Appa Balwant Chowk, Opp. Prabhat Talkies, Pune - 411 030.
Ph. 24434662.Mobile: 9325315464.

Printed at
Success Publications
S.No. 30/27, Laxmi Industrial Estate, Near Prabhat News Paper,
Dhayari, Pune-41.Mobile : 9028211751

Edition
2019

Edited By
Mr. Valmik Gaikwad

Typesetting, Layout
Mrs. Aparna Mali

Cover Designing
Mrs. Aparna Mali

ISBN NO. – 978-93-89066-80-7

Preface

This is the great satisfaction that we are presenting this book of Business Economics (Micro) for F.Y.B.Com.

Writing is always a challenge. If you were ever challenged to express yourself via the written word, this book is for you. Writing for Success is a text that provides instruction in steps, builds writing, reading, and critical thinking.

This book can cover entire given syllabus and in can give you satisfaction of enough study. We assure you that this book will clear all concepts of Business Economics.

Features of this Book :

- ➢ This book addresses each concept with clear, concise, and effective examples that are immediately reinforced with exercises.
- ➢ Each chapter allows students to demonstrate mastery of the principles of quality writing.
- ➢ This book will not only help to write the answers but also to clear concept of the subjects.
- ➢ This book can improve a range of writing levels and abilities of students
- ➢ We have given point wise explanation of every chapter which will help you to understand chapter properly.
- ➢ Each chapter also has integrated examples that unify the discussion.

We are very grateful to Mrs. Dr. Saroj Hiremath Madam (Vice Principal), Mr. Dr. Pravin Ransure Sir (HOD, Economics Dept., Dr. Ambedkar Scholar) and Mr. Ramdas Gadage Sir (HOD, Business Economics and Banking) for giving opportunity to writing this Book. We are also thankful to our publisher Mr. Rajesh Patne who provided all assistants to bring this book in market.

Suggestions of readers are welcome and shall be acknowledged with gratitude.

With best wishes. ***By Authors***

Syllabus

F.Y.B.Com. (Sem. - I)

Business Economics – I (Micro)

Unit No.	Tital and Contents	No. of Lectures = 48
1	**INTRODUCTION** **1.1** Business Economic: Introduction **1.2** Two Major Branches of Business Economics – (a) Microeconomics (b) Macroeconomics **1.3** Meaning of Business Economics – Micro **1.4** Scope and Importance of Business economics (Micro) **1.5** Limitations of Microeconomics	10
2	**TOOLS AND GOALS OF FIRMS** **2.1** Tools for Analysis **A)** Functional Relationships **B)** Schedules **C)** Graphs **D)** Equations **2.2** Goals of Firms :Economic and Non-economics	08
3	**DEMAND ANALYSIS** **3.1** Utility approach : Cardinal and Ordinal **3.2** Law of Diminishing Marginal Utility **3.3** Law of Demand **3.4** Concept of Elasticity of Demand Types of Elasticity of Demand	15

	3.5 Consumer Behavior - Indifference Curve Analysis : Concept of Income, Substitution and Price Effect **3.6** Consumer Equilibrium **3.7** Consumer surplus **3.8** Demand Estimation and Demand Forecasting- Meaning and objectives Methods of Demand Estimation - Descriptive Analysis Methods of Demand Forecasting - Descriptive analysis	
4	**PRODUCTION AND COST ANALYSIS** **4.1** Supply - Law of supply **4.2** Production Function **4.3(a)**Law of Variable Proportions - The Three Stages **(b)**Law of Returns to Scale - The Three Stages **(c)**Economies and Diseconomies of Scale – Internal & External **4.6**Cost Analysis **(A)** Concept of Costs **(B)** Behavior of Cost Curves **1.** Short Run **2.** Long Run	15

INDEX

F.Y.B.Com. (Sem. - I)

Business Economics – I (Micro)

INTRODUCTION

UNIT 1

1.1 Business Economics : Introduction :

Business economics is a field in applied economics which uses economic theory and quantitative methods to examine business enterprises and the factors contributing to the diversity of organizational structures and the relationships of firms with labour, capital and product market.

Economics is the study of choice under conditions of scarcity. This definition has two parts a) choice and b) scarcity. Scarcity is a situation in which the amount of something available is insufficient to satisfy the desire for it. As an individual, for instance, we face scarcity of time and spending power. Given more or either, we could have more of goods and services that we desire. at any given point of time, individuals face numerous scarcities. There are so many things one might like to have – sedan cars, branded clothes, shoes, branded watches, sport equipment, studio apartments, and so on……i.e., individuals have unlimited wants but face the constraint of limited spending power.

Business Economics uses microeconomics analysis of business unit and macroeconomics analysis of the business environment. Microeconomics is used to evaluate the performance of a business unit and business manager's position therein. It foresees its attention mainly on individual units like a consumer, a producer, a firm or a single commodity. It helps us to understand the behaviour of a single thing. In macroeconomics analysis, we study the system as a whole, not the individuals but the total.

1.2 Two major branches of Business Economics :

(A) Microeconomic

(B) Macroeconomics

In our daily lives, we face innumerable economic decisions, such as choosing what to buy with available money or what to do during our free time. These topics, which are related to the decisions of **individual agents** (individuals, families, businesses), are the object of study in an area of economics called **microeconomics.** Microeconomics may be defined as that branch of economic analysis which studies the economic behaviour of individual unit, may be a person, a particular household, or particular firm. It is a study of one particular unit rather than all the units combined together.

The microeconomics is also described as the price and value theory, the theory of the household, the firm and the industry. Most production and welfare theories are of microeconomics verity.

Another area of economics is **macroeconomics,** which studies the relationship between economic **aggregates**. Economic aggregates are elements that are made up of the sum of other variables. Or macroeconomics may be defined as the branches of economic analysis which studies behaviour of not one particular unit but of all the units combined together. It is a study in aggregates. Hence, it is often called Aggregative Economics.

For instance, the Gross Domestic Product (GDP) is the sum of everything that is produced by each individual and organization within a country. The consumer price index is made up of the average price of numerous products. The aggregate investment is the sum of the expenditures in investment of all businesses and families of a country, etc.

5.3.1 Difference between Micro and Macro Economics :

Points of Comparison	Microeconomics	Macroeconomics
Meaning	It takes into account small components of whole economy.	It takes into consideration the economy of any country as a whole.
Definition	It's a branch of economics which deals with the economic decision-making of individual economic agents such as producer, the consumer, etc...	It's a branch of economics which deals with aggregates and averages of the entire economy, e.g., Aggregate output, national income, aggregate savings and investment, etc..

Nature	It is the study of individual units in particular, consumer, firm and resource owners.	It is a study of the behaviour of the economy as a whole.
Methodology	Microeconomics is individualistic approach. It's a slicing method.	Macroeconomics is aggregative approach. It studies by lumping method.
Economic variables	Microeconomics is concerned with the behaviour of micro variables such as individual demand, supply, wages, etc.	Macroeconomics pertains to the problem of the size of national income economic growth and general price level.
Basis	Price mechanism is the basis of microeconomics.	Income mechanism is the basis of macroeconomics.
Analysis	Microeconomics considered as a static analysis.	Macroeconomics is considered as dynamic analysis.
Scope	Its scope is limited as it never uses the aggregates relating to the economy, wide total.	It uses the aggregates which relates to the entire economy.
Objective	The main objective of microeconomics is to maximize utility by consumers (demand side) and maximize profits by firms (on supply side).	The main objective of macroeconomics is full employment, economic growth, price stability and favorable balance of payments.
Economist	Prof. Marshall's magnum opus, "principles of Economics" (1890) dealt in detail with microeconomics.	J.M. Keynes celebrated work, general theory of employment, interest and money" (1936) is an outstanding work of macroeconomics approach.

1.3 Meaning of Business Economics – micro :

3.1.1. Meaning :

The term Micro has been borrowed from the Greek word, 'Mikros' meaning small. But it may not be misunderstood that micro economics refers to small or insignificant economics. As a matter of fact micro economics is as much important as macro-economics. According to Bilas, "The term micro in economics means division into small parts of such economic variables as consumption, investment, saving, etc. "under Micro economics, we study individual units, like, a consumer, a firm, an industry, price determination of a particular commodity etc. We also study 'group' in it. For example, market demand curve, which is the aggregate of individual demand curve, is also a subject of study of Micro economics, but we do not study in it large or national-level groups. Composition and allocation of total production fall under the scope of microeconomics study, whereas under macro economics we study level of aggregate production.

3.1.2. Definitions :

1) **Watson :**

   "Micro economics is the theory of the small, of the behaviour of the consumers, producers and markets."

2) **Shaplro :**

   "Micro economics deals with small parts of the economy."

3) **Left witch :**

   "Micro economics concerned with the economic activities of economic units as consumers, resources owners and business firms."

4) **Boulding :**

   "Micro economics is the study of particular firm, particular household, individual price, wages, income, industry and particular commodity."

1.4 Scope and importance of business economics – Micro :

1.4.1 Scope of Microeconomics :

1) **Theory of demand :**

   It studies how the demand for a commodity is determined and what is the law of demand. Theory of demand refers to the demand of consumer and his maximum satisfaction. It studies how a consumer distributes his limited income on the purchase of different goods at different prices so as to get maximum satisfaction.

2) **Theory of production :**

   It also studies the theory relating to production of goods. A firm Carrie's out production with the help of factors of production. Under theory of production one studies production function and the laws governing production of goods.

3) **The theory of price determination :**

   Micro economics also deals with the theory of price determination. Besides analysing the conditions of demand and supply, theory of price determination seeks to explain how the prices of goods produced under different market conditions, such as, perfect market, monopoly etc. is determined, condition of demand and supply are also studied in this theory.

4) Theory of factor pricing :

Income received by the sale of goods produced with the help of different factors of production, is distributed among these factors in the form of factor-price, viz., rent, wages, interest and profit. How price of each factors of production is determined is a problem that deals with distribution of income and so is studied under micro economics.

5) Optimum Allocation of resources :

Micro economics is also concerned with the optimum allocation of resources that is how efficiently resources are distributed among the consumers and producers. A consumer or a firm is in equilibrium when there is optimum allocation of resources. Micro Economics therefore studies the conditions necessary for achieving equilibrium.

6) Welfare Economics :

Micro economics also studies welfare economics. It spells out an ideal economy. It deals with the welfare of the people as consumers and producers.

1.4.2 Importance of Microeconomics :

1) For price determination :

Microeconomics explains how prices of various products and those of factors of production (productive services) are determined in the product market and factor market respectively.

2) Allocation of resources :

Microeconomics explains how millions of consumers and producers in an economy take decisions about the allocation of productive resources among various goods and services.

3) Working of free enterprise economy :

Microeconomics explains the functioning of a free enterprise economy. It tells us how millions of consumers and firm operate independently of each other, but at the same time are able to ensure the smooth functioning of the economic system.

4) For decision making :

Microeconomics helps in decision-making in business. The businessman can determine the cost of production and estimate the demand for his product. It helps a businessman in the attainment of maximum productivity through optimum allocation of resources.

5) Market structure :

Microeconomics provides a framework to study different kinds of market structure like perfect competition, monopoly, oligopoly, etc.

6) For welfare :

It serves as the basis for welfare economics. It suggests how to maximize welfare of the consumers and eliminate wastage and have optimisation of resources so as to fetch maximum social welfare.

7) International trade :

It explains many aspects of international trade such as emergency, nature and gains of international trade, determination of exchange rate, etc.

Micro economics models help to describe the actual economic situation and also suggest policies that bring about desired result.

1.5 Limitations of microeconomics :

1) Unrealistic assumptions :

Micro economics is based on unrealistic assumptions, especially in case of full employment, laissez faire assumption which do not exist in reality. Even the behaviour of an individual cannot be generalised as the behaviour of all. Hence economic laws cannot be universally true.

2) Cetris paribus :

It assumes that all other things remain constant [equal or same] but actually it is not so.

3) Pure capitalism :

Micro economics unrealistically assumes laissez faire policy or pure capitalism. This means it assumes non-intervention of the government. It was due to this that it could not provide a proper solution for the depression of 1930's.

4) Inadequate data :

Micro economics is based on the information dealing with individual behaviour. Hence it is difficult to get correct information. What is true for an individual unit may not be true in case of aggregates eg as Lord J M Keynes says, “individual saving is a virtue, but national saving may prove a calamity”. Therefore because of incorrect data, micro economics may provide inaccurate results.

5) Marginalism :

Marginal means the impact of an additional unit. Micro economics uses concepts like marginal utility, marginal product, marginal revenue etc. However it is difficult to realize the principle of marginalism in real life.

6) National problem ignored :

Micro economics does not deal with the national problems like business cycles inflation etc. which are important problems for the nation.

7) Help of macro economics :

Micro economics has to take some help of macroeconomics, particularly for explaining determination of profit and rate of interest. These limitations do not mean that the study of the micro economics is not useful, its study is very important in all fields of economics.

Points to Remember

❖ **Business Economics : Introduction**

Business economics is a field in applied economics which uses economic theory and quantitative methods to examine business enterprises and the factors contributing to the diversity of organizational structures and the relationships of firms with labour, capital and product market.

❖ **Two major branches of Business Economics :**

(A) Microeconomic

(B) Macroeconomics

In our daily lives, we face innumerable economic decisions, such as choosing what to buy with available money or what to do during our free time. These topics, which are related to the decisions of **individual agents** (individuals, families, businesses), are the object of study in an area of economics called **microeconomics.**

Macroeconomics may be defined as the branches of economic analysis which studies behaviour of not one particular unit but of all the units combined together. It is a study in aggregates. Hence, it is often called Aggregative Economics.

❖ **Difference between Micro and Macro Economics**

❖ **Meaning of Business Economics – micro**

▪ **Meaning :**

The term Micro has been borrowed from the Greek word, 'Mikros' meaning small. According to Bilas, "The term micro in economics means division into small parts of such economic variables as consumption, investment, saving, etc." under Micro economics, we study individual units, like, a consumer, a firm, an industry, price determination of a particular commodity etc.

▪ **Definitions**

➤ **Watson :**

"Micro economics is the theory of the small, of the behaviour of the consumers, producers and markets."

➤ **Shaplro :**

"Micro economics deals with small parts of the economy."

➤ **Left witch :**

Micro economics concerned with the economic activities of economic units as consumers, resources owners and business firms.

➤ **Boulding :**

"Micro economics is the study of particular firm, particular household, individual price, wages, income, industry and particular commodity."

❖ **scope and importance of business economics – Micro**

❖ **scope of Microeconomics :**

- Theory of demand
- Theory of production
- The theory of price determination
- Theory of factor pricing
- Optimum Allocation of resources
- Welfare Economics

❖ **importance of microeconomics :**

- For price determination
- Allocation of resources
- Working of free enterprise economy
- For decision making
- Market structure
- For welfare
- International trade

❖ **limitations of microeconomics :**

- Unrealistic assumptions
- Cetris paribus
- Pure capitalism
- Inadequate data
- Marginalism
- National problem ignored
- Help of macro economics

Questions for discussion

1) What is mean by Business Economics?
2) Define Business Economics –micro.
3) What is microeconomics?
4) Explain the scope of business economics.
5) Distinguish between Microeconomics and Macroeconomics.
6) Describe the importance of Microeconomics.
7) State the limitations of Microeconomics.

Tools and goal of firm

UNIT 2

2.1 Tools for analysis

2.2 Goals of Firms : Economic and Non – Economic

2.1 Tools for analysis :

In this section we will describe and illustrate the use of some important mathematical tools of analysis often used in economics and business decision-making.

A) Functional relationship :

Economics is all about relationships of mankind and nature, relationships of individuals you one another. The laws of diminishing marginal utility or diminishing returns or supply and demands are all statements of those relationships, which we can use to predict or explain economic matters. There are many variables used in economic laws. Some kind of relation can exist between two or more variables.

- **The Function**

A function is a mathematical technique of stating symbolically that there exist relationships between any two or more variables. For example, suppose two variables, X and Y, are so related that the value of Y depends on the value of X. The relationship between X and Y is then expressed in the functional form as:

$$Y= f(X)$$

Above equation is read as Y is a function of X. It means that value of Y depends on the value of X and that for each value of X, there is a unique value of Y.

Hence variable Y is called as dependent variable and X is called as independent variable.

E.g., the relationship between the variables such as demand and income or demand and price is called as functional relationship. It can be direct or inverse. Price and supply are directly related. There is inverse relationship between price and demand for a commodity. It can be expressed as,

Demand = f (price)

Individual demand for a commodity can be expressed mathematically in the general functional form Qd = f(price, income, tastes, etc.). Variable on the left hand side is dependent variable and variable on right hand side are independent variables. Sometimes demand schedule or supply schedule is also called demand function and supply function respectively.

B) Schedule :

Basically Schedule in economic means a table or chart showing relationship between two variable. For eg. In a supply schedule, we will have different prices of a commodity and units of that commodity, which the seller is willing to supply. Similarly, we can have aggregate demand schedule, aggregate supply schedule, etc.

E.g.

Price of the quantity	Quantity demanded	Quantity supplied
0	20	-10
1	18	-8
2	16	-6
3	14	-4
4	12	-2
5	10	0
6	8	2
7	6	4
7.5	5	5
8	4	6
9	2	8
10	0	10
11	-2	12
12	-4	14

(Relationship between price, demand and supply of quantity)

The table shows that with changing price of quantity the quantity demanded and quantity supplied are also changes.

C) Graphs :

Graph is simple representation of relation between two economic variables. The depiction of functional relationship through schedule is simple enough, but economists usually prefer to represent these relationships through graphs or equations. This is because schedule shows the relationship only between specific quantities and prices or specific data of any kind. Graphs and equations show generalized relationship, relationship that covers all quantities and prices or all values of any two things we are interested in.

The simplest and most intuitively obvious method of showing a functional relationship is through a graph. The above price, demand and supply of quantity showing schedule can be graphically represented as follows:

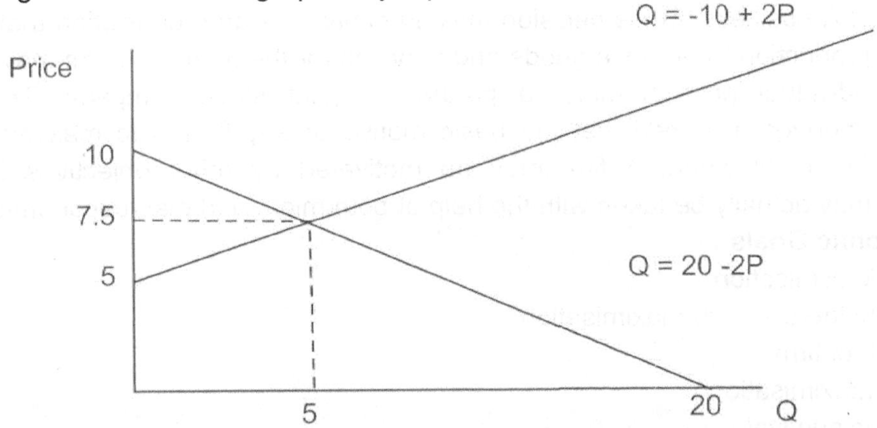

Above graph showing the relationship between price and quantity demanded with the help demand and supply curve.

D) Equations :

Equation is an important way of representing functional relations and is often used for its simplicity and brevity. Equations are very convenient means of representing functional relationships, science they allow us to consider the impact of more than one factor at a time. The typical equation for demand might look like this

Qd = f(P)

Equations are used for explaining various economic factors and law. It also used to balance two different quantities.

Let us suppose we have two simple supply and demand equations

1) Qd = 20 – 2P

2) Qs = -10 + 2P

To find where Qs = Qd we put two equations together

20 – 2P = -10 + 2P

20 + 10 = 4P

30/4 = P

P = 7.5

To find Q, we just put this value of P into one of the equations

Q = 20 – (2 × 7.5)

Q = 5

Thus if the price were ? **7.5** then buyers would take **5 units.**

2.2 Goals of Firms : Economic and Non – Economic :

A firm is a collection of resources that is transformed into products demanded by consumers. A business firm is decision making entity. It is an organization that employs factors of production to produce goods and services for the market. A firm may be in the form of individual proprietorship, a partner or joint stock company. Traditionally economic theories assumed that the basic motive of any firm is to maximize profits. However in actual world, a firm may be motivated by other objectives for which decisions may actually be taken with the help of both micro and macroeconomics.

A) Economic Goals :

a. Profit Maximisation
b. Shareholders wealth maximisation
c. Growth of firm
d. Sales maximisation
e. long run survival

B) Non - economic Goals :

a. Political power and prestige
b. Social responsibility and welfare
c. Goodwill of employees

A) Economic Goals :

1) Profit Maximisation:

A process that companies undergo to determine the best output and price levels in order to maximize its return. The company will usually adjust influential factors such as production costs, sale prices, and output levels as a way of reaching its profit goal. There are two main profit maximization methods used, and they are Marginal Cost-Marginal Revenue Method and Total Cost-Total Revenue Method.

Profit = Total Revenue – Total Cost

- **For profit maximisation two conditions should be fulfil :**

1. Marginal Revenue must be equal to the marginal cost.
   MR = MC (necessary condition)
2. Marginal cost curve should cut marginal revenue curve from the below.

- Marginal cost (MC) = It is a cost arising due to the production of one additional unit of output.
- Marginal revenue (MR) = It is the revenue obtained from the production and sale of one additional unit of output.

The conditions are illustrated by point P2 in the following figure :

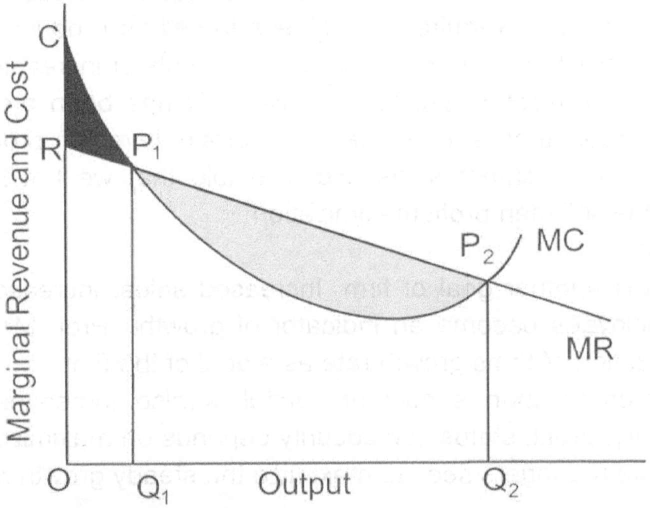

(Marginal condition of profit maximisation)

2) Shareholders wealth maximization :

These are the individuals, businesses, and institutions that have an ownership interest in a company after purchasing shares of that company's stock. Even if your business is a one-person shop, you are the shareholder because of your invested interest in your company. Because shareholders own the firm, they are entitled to the profits of the firm.

Shareholder wealth is the appropriate goal of a business firm in a capitalist society. In a capitalist society, there is private ownership of goods and services by individuals. Those individuals own the means of production to make money. The profits from the businesses in the economy accrue to the individuals.

When business managers try to maximize the wealth of their firm, they are actually trying to increase the company's stock price. As the stock price increases, the value of the firm increases, as well as the shareholders' wealth.

3) Sales maximization :

When it comes to business, maximizing sales and profits are two fundamental objectives. Sales maximization is a business strategy that a company implements when it wants to focus on generating as much revenue as possible. Profit maximization is the objective of generating as much profit as possible over time. Sales are the initial steps toward profitability. There are no profits without sales. A business must choose to focus on maximizing either its revenue or profits, but it typically cannot do both at the same time. Revenue measures the amount of income a business generates through the sale of its products or services, while profit measures the income remaining after costs, expenses and taxes are taken out.

Revenue maximization often involves reducing prices to increase the total number of sales. Maximizing profits requires a business to sell its products or services at the highest possible profit margin, by either reducing costs or increasing prices.

Sales revenue maximization principle of oligopoly has been propounded by w . J Baumol. He argues that a firm seeks a certain level of profit and within that constraint aims at maximum sales. He also told that we have to give the more importance to the sell than profit maximization.

4) Growth of firm :

Growth of firm is another goal of firm. Increased sales, increased assets, growing number of employees become an indicator of growth. Prof. Morris suggested the goal of maximization of firms growth rate as a goal of the firm.

If demand increases then supply of capital is also increases. Maximization of variable as salary, profit, status, job security depends on maximization of growth rate of firm. Therefore managers seek to maximize the steady growth rate.

Limitations :

a. It fails to deal satisfactory with oligopolistic market. Where the firms behavior is interdependent.

b. It ignores price mechanism.

5) Long - run survival

K W Rothschild suggested suggested this goal of firm. Under this objective the firm seeks to maximize the probability of its survival into the future. By providing security, insurance for the future generation. Also by building policy as strong pillar for the long run survival. Management aims at this objective because their present and future compensation depends upon the firms survival. Managers would not prefer their firms to be short-lived or become bankrupt. For achieving this objective of long run survival or continuity of existence, business decision is made in such a way that risk are avoided or minimized.

Unlike other objective of firms, the objective of long-run survival is hard to measure and difficult to practice.

- **Non-economic goal of firm :**

1) Political power :

In democracy, political parties and elections are inevitable many industrialists or businessman have a desire to back a particular political party and to acquire political importance. Power and politics introduction power is important within organizations because power is the way in which management influences individuals to make things happen.

2) Social responsibility and welfare :

It is very important non-economic goal of firm. It Willingness to advance goal of groups like employees, suppliers, local community, non-government organization society. Workers should be provided good working condition, insurance, good wages and other benefits increases social welfare in particular industry.

3) **Goodwill of employees :**

Developing good relation with employees is characteristics of small firms and the large sized firms are de-private of this facility. Facility like – providing quarters, medical care, schooling facility, many schemes helps creating good will in the employees. This will make the firm strong, healthy and successful.

Points to Remember

- **Tools for analysis**

In this section we will describe and illustrate the use of some important mathematical tools of analysis often used in economics and business decision-making.

A) Functional relationship :

- **The Function :**

A function is a mathematical technique of stating symbolically that there exist relationships between any two or more variables.

For example, **Y= f(X)**

Above equation is read as Y is a function of X. It means that value of Y depends on the value of X and that for each value of X, there is a unique value of Y.

Hence variable Y is called as dependent variable and X is called as independent variable.

E.g., the relationship between the variables such as demand and income or demand and price is called as functional relationship.

B) Schedule :

Basically Schedule in economic means a table or chart showing relationship between two variable. For eg. In a supply schedule, we will have different prices of a commodity and units of that commodity, which the seller is willing to supply.

C) Graphs :

Graph is simple representation of relation between two economic variables. The simplest and most intuitively obvious method of showing a functional relationship is through a graph.

D) Equations :

Equation is an important way of representing functional relations and is often used for its simplicity and brevity. Equations are very convenient means of representing functional relationships, science they allow us to consider the impact of more than one factor at a time.

- **Goals of Firms : Economic and Non – Economic :**

A business firm is decision making entity. It is an organization that employs factors of production to produce goods and services for the market. Traditionally economic theories assumed that the basic motive of any firm is to maximize profits. However in actual world, a firm may be motivated by other objectives for which decisions may actually be taken with the help of both micro and macroeconomics.

A) Economic Goals :

1. Profit Maximisation:

A process that companies undergo to determine the best output and price levels in order to maximize its return.

Profit = Total Revenue – Total Cost

- **For profit maximisation two conditions should be fulfil :**

1) Marginal Revenue must be equal to the marginal cost.
MR = MC (necessary condition)

2) Marginal cost curve should cut marginal revenue curve from the below.

- Marginal cost (MC) = It is a cost arising due to the production of one additional unit of output.
- Marginal revenue (MR) = It is the revenue obtained from the production and sale of one additional unit of output.

3) Shareholders wealth maximization :

Shareholder wealth is the appropriate goal of a business firm in a capitalist society. In a capitalist society, there is private ownership of goods and services by individuals. Those individuals own the means of production to make money. The profits from the businesses in the economy accrue to the individuals.

4) Sales maximization :

Sales maximization is a business strategy that a company implements when it wants to focus on generating as much **revenue** as possible.

Sales revenue maximization principle of oligopoly has been propounded by w . J Baumol.

5) Growth of firm :

Prof. Morris suggested the goal of maximization of firms growth rate as a goal of the firm.

If demand increases then supply of capital is also increases. Maximization of variable as salary, profit, status, job security depends on maximization of growth rate of firm. Therefore managers seek to maximize the steady growth rate.

Limitations :

a. It fails to deal satisfactory with oligopolistic market.

b. It ignores price mechanism.

6) Long - run survival :

K W Rothschild suggested suggested this goal of firm. Under this objective the firm seeks to maximize the probability of its survival into the future. By providing security, insurance for the future generation. Also by building policy as strong pillar for the long run survival.

- **Non-economic goal of firm :**

1) Political power
2) Social responsibility and welfare
3) Goodwill of employees

Questions for discussion

1) Explain the Tools for Analysis used by economists.
2) What are functional relationships?
3) What is a Function?
4) What are Equations?
5) What is Schedule?
6) What are graphs?
7) Explain the Economic Goals of Firm.
8) State the Non-Economic Goals of Firms.
9) Explain each of the Economic and Non-Economic Goals of Firms.

DEMAND ANALYSIS

UNIT 3

Introduction :

In explaining consumer behavior, consumer chooses those goods and services which gives high value. Consumer chooses one commodity among different commodities which develop notion of utility.

3.1 Utility Approach :

- **Meaning of utility :**

  What do you mean by **"utility"**? In a word, utility denotes satisfaction. It refers how consumer ranks different goods and services. If commodity A having higher utility than commodity B, consumer will prefer commodity A over B.

  In other word "power of commodity which satisfy human want, is called utility." It means if any commodity or unit of commodity which fulfills consumer's need, we can say utility is there in commodity or in unit of commodity.

➢ THE CARDINAL AND ORDINAL UTILITY APPROACH

INTRODUCTIN

The cardinal or neo–classical utility analysis refers to the theory of consumer demand as built by Marshal, Pigou and others. This theory is based on the cordial measurement of utility which assumes that utility is measurable in numerical form and addictive. It is expressed as a quantity measured in hypothetical units, which are called 'utile'. If a consumer imagines that one mango has 8 utile and an apple 4 utils, it implies that the utility of one mango is that of an apple.

➢ ASSUMPTION OF CARDINAL UTILITY ANALYSIS :

The utility analysis is based on a set of following assumption:

1) The utility analysis is based on the cardinal concept which assumes that utility is measurable and addictive like weights and lengths of goods.
2) Utility is measurable in terms of money.
3) The marginal utility of money is assumed to be constant.
4) The consumer is rational who measures, calculates, chooses and compares the utilities of different units of the various commodities and aims at the maximization of utility.
5) He has full knowledge of the availability of commodities and their technical qualities.
6) He possesses perfect knowledge of the choice of commodities open to him and his choices are certain.
7) He knows the exact prices of various commodities and their utilities are not influence by variations in their prices.
8) There are no substitutes.

➢ List of concepts which are based on Cardinal concept :

1) The entire Marshallian analysis, comprising
2) The Law of Diminishing Marginal Utility,
3) The Law of Maximum Satisfaction,
4) The concept of Consumer's Surplus
5) The Law of Demand

➢ ORDINAL UTILITY APPROACH :

The modern economists have discarded the concept of cardinal utility and instead applied ordinal utility approach to study the behavior of the consumers. While the neo-classical economists believed that the utility can be measured and expressed in cardinal numbers, but the modern economists maintain that the utility being the psychological phenomena cannot be measured theoretically, quantitatively and even cardinally.

Meaning of Ordinal utility

The **Ordinal Utility** is based on the fact that the utility of a commodity cannot be measured in numerical term, but however, it can be proved that utility derived from commodity may be more, less or equal by comparing two or more commodities. This concept is given by J R Hicks and Allen.

➢ The ordinal utility theory or the indifference curve analysis is based on four main assumptions.

i) Rational behavior of the consumer: It is assumed that individuals are rational in making decisions from their expenditures on consumer goods.

ii) Utility is ordinal: Utility cannot be measured cardinally. It can be, however, expressed ordinally. In other words, the consumer can rank the basket of goods according to the satisfaction or utility of each basket.

iii) Consistency in choice: The consumer, it is assumed, is consistent in his behavior during a period of time. For insistence, if the consumer prefers combinations of A of good to the combinations B of goods, he then remains consistent in his choice. His preference, during another period of time does not change. Symbolically, it can be expressed as:

If A > B, then B > A

iv) Consumer's preference not self contradictory: The consumer's preferences are not self contradictory. It means that if combinations A is preferred over combination B is preferred over C, then combination A is preferred over combination A is preferred over C. Symbolically it can be expressed:

If A > B and B > C, then A > C

v) Goods consumed are substitutable: The goods consumed by the consumer are substitutable. The utility can be maintained at the same level by consuming more of some goods and less of the other. There are many combinations of the two commodities which are equally preferred by a consumer and he is indifferent as to which of the two he receives.

➢ **List of concepts which are based on Ordinal concept :**

1) Indifference curve

2) Budget line

3) Equilibrium by indifference curve and budget line

➢ **Concept of total utility and marginal utility :**

Total utility

Utility derived from all the units of commodity, is called total utility.

$$\textbf{Total Utility} = MU_1 + MU_2 + MU_3 \ldots\ldots + MU_{nth}$$

Marginal utility

Utility derived from every additional unit of commodity is called marginal utility. Or change in total utility due consumption of one more unit.

$$\textbf{Marginal Utility} = TU_n - TU_{n-1}$$

- **Relationship of Total utility and Marginal utility:**

  Look at the below-given schedule and diagram, to understand three important relationships between total utility and marginal utility:

Units of comodity	Total utility	Marginal utility
1	30	30
2	56	26
3	76	20
4	88	12
5	90	2
6	90	0
7	86	-4
8	78	-8

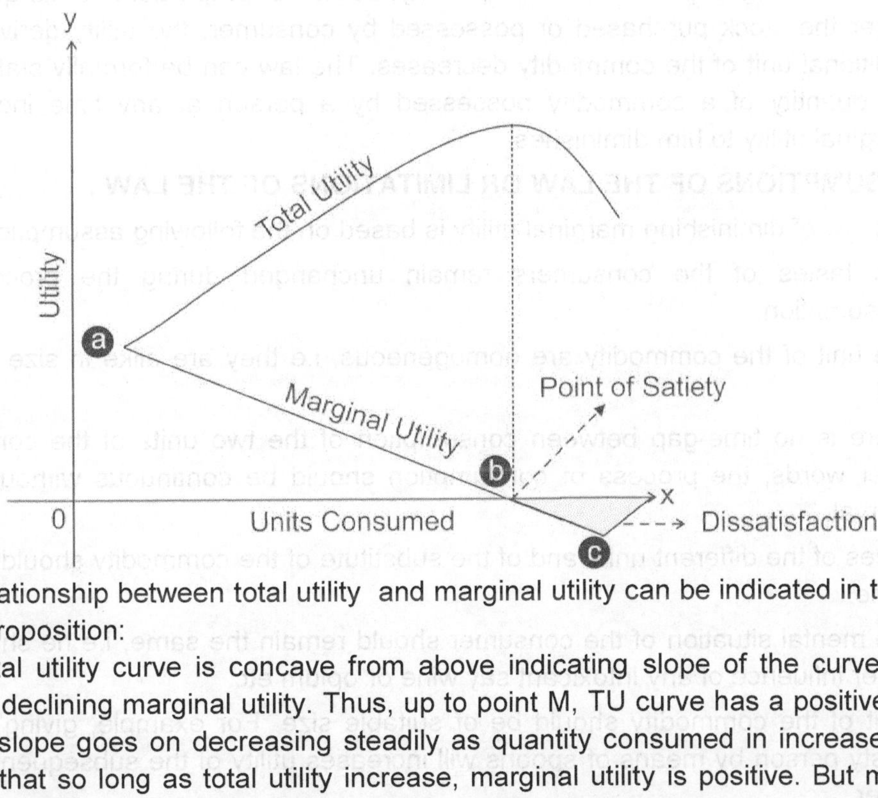

- The relationship between total utility and marginal utility can be indicated in terms of three proposition:

1) The total utility curve is concave from above indicating slope of the curve, which means declining marginal utility. Thus, up to point M, TU curve has a positive slope, but its slope goes on decreasing steadily as quantity consumed in increased. This shows that so long as total utility increase, marginal utility is positive. But marginal utility decrease because total utility increase at a decreasing rate.
2) When total utility is maximum, marginal utility is zero. When total utility curve reaches its maximum (at point M), its slope is zero, which is another way of saying that marginal utility is zero.

After M, the slope of total utility curve becomes negative showing that the marginal utility is negative. Thus, when total utility decline marginal utility is negative.

3.2 Law of DMU :

This law is given by Alfred Marshal in his book "Principle of Economics".

- **Statement of Law :**

  "The law states that as the consumer consumes units of commodity one by one, utility derived from every additional unit i.e. marginal utility keeps on decreases."

- **Meaning of marginal utility :**

  "Utility derived from every additional unit of commodity."

  According to this law, as the person purchases more and more units of a commodity, it's marginal utility declines. The law points out that the marginal utility of the commodity depends upon its quantity, but is not proportional to its quantity. The larger the stock purchased or possessed by consumer, the utility derived from an additional unit of the commodity decreases. The law can be formally stated thus, as the quantity of a commodity possessed by a person at any time increases, it's marginal utility to him diminishes.

- **ASSUMPTIONS OF THE LAW OR LIMITATIONS OF THE LAW :**

  The law of diminishing marginal utility is based on the following assumption,:

- The tastes of the consumers remain unchanged during the process of the consumption.
- The unit of the commodity are homogeneous, i.e they are alike in size and quality and,
- There is no time-gap between consumption of the two units of the commodity. In other words, the process of consumption should be continuous without any time-interval.
- Prices of the different units and of the substitute of the commodity should remain the same.
- The mental situation of the consumer should remain the same, i.e he should not be under influence of any intoxicant say wine or oplum etc.
- Unit of the commodity should be of suitable size. For example, giving water to a thirsty person by means of spoons will increases utility of the subsequent spoons of water.
- The taste, habits, fashion, temperament and the income of the consumer should remain the same.
- Explanation of Law

Units of commodity	Marginal utility
1	10
2	8
3	6
4	4
5	2
6	0
7	-2

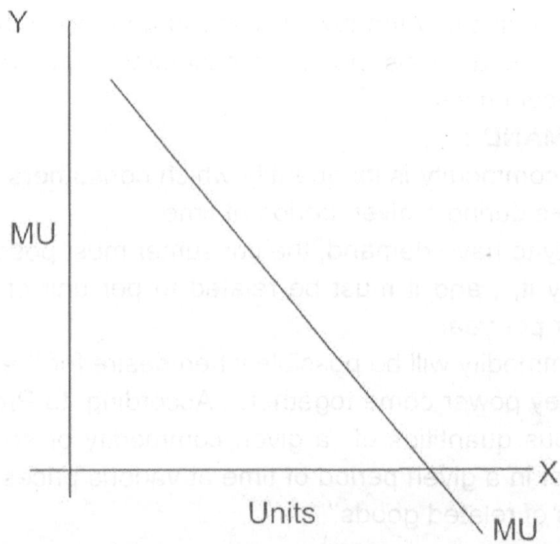

Explanation of schedule :

In given schedule, as the consumer consumes units of commodity one by one, utility derived from every additional unit i.e. marginal utility decreases. At certain level it becomes zero and it will be consumer's equilibrium point. No rational consumer will go beyond this point, because the marginal utility becomes negative which will disequilibrium for consumer.

Explanation of Diagram :

In given diagram the MU curve slops left to right downward because as the consumer increases unites of commodity, MU decreases which shows inverse relation between units and MU. Then it touches to X axis and then become negative.

➢ **Exceptions to the Law of Diminishing Marginal Utility :**

1) It is pointed out that the consumption of liquor is not subject to the law of diminishing marginal utility. The more a person drinks liquor, the More be likes it. In other words, it is said that the marginal utility of liquor increased consumption.

2) It is pointed out that the law of diminishing Marginal utility does not apply to money .The more money a person has the greater is the desire to acquire still more of a this is particularly true in the case of a money. But even the miser is subject in the opctatum of the law in the long run.

3) It is pointed out that such hobbies as collection of stamps, old paintings, coins, old glass and so forth offer an exception to the law of diminishing marginal utility .Greater the collections of a person, greater is his desire to acquire additional units of these commodities.

3.3 Law of Demand:

- **DEMAND ANALYSIS :**

In this chapter, we shall study the law of demand and the in the next the elasticity of demand. But before we analysis them, it is essential to understand the nature of the term 'Demand' in economics.

- **MEANING OF DEMAND :**

The demand for a commodity is its quantity which consumers are willing and able to buy at various prices during a given period of time.

So, far a commodity to have demand, the consumer must possess willingness to buy it, the ability to buy it, , and it must be related to per unit of time I.e. per day, per week, per month or per year.

So Demand for commodity will be possible when desire for the commodity and ability to pay means money power come together. According to Prof. Bober ,"By demand we mean the various quantities of a given commodity or service which consumes would buy in market in a given period of time at various prices or at various incomes or at various prices of related goods"

- **Demand Functions :**

The demand functions are an algebraic expression of the relationship between demand for a community and its various determinants that affect this quantity.

i) Individual Demand Functions :

An individual's demand function refers to the quantities of demanded at various prices, given his income, prices of related goods and tastes. It is expressed as

$$D = f(p)$$

ii) Market Demand Function :

An individual demand function is the basis of demand theory. But it is the market demand function that is main interest to manager's .It refers to the total demand for a good or service of all the buyers taken together. The market demand function may be expressed mathematically thus

$$D=f(px, py, M, T, A.U)$$

➢ THE LAW OF DEMAND :

Statement of Law

"Law of demand states that other factors being constant, the quantity of commodity increases when price decreases and the quantity of commodity decreases when price increases."

Defined in Marshall's words as "the amount demanded increases with a fall in price, and diminishes with a rise in price in price ".Thus it expresses an inverse relation between price and demand. The law refers to the direction in which quantity demanded changes with a change in price. On the figure, it is represented by the slope of the demand curve which is normally negative throughout its length. The inverse price-demand relationship is based on other things remaining equal. This phrase points towards certain important assumptions on which this law is based.

➢ Its Assumptions :

These assumptions are:

i) There are no changes in the taste and preferences of the consumer

ii) The income of the consumer remains constant;

iii) There is no change in customs;

iv) The commodity to be used should nor confer distinction on the consumer,

v) There should not be any substitute of the commodity;

vi) There should not be any change in the prices of other procedure;

vii) There should not be any possibility of changes in the price of the product being used;

viii) There should not be any change in the quality of the product and

ix) The habits of the consumers should remain unchanged. Given these conditions, the law of demand operates. If there is change even in one of these conditions, it will stop operating.

Demand Schedule

Price	Quantity
100	10
80	20
60	30
40	40

Above table shows that when the price of commodity is Rs. 100 per unit, 10 units are demanded. If the price falls to Rs.80, the demand increases to 20 units. Similarly, when the price declines to Rs.60, the demand increases to 30 units.

Demand Curve

In the figure point p of the demand curves DD, shows demand for Q units at the Rs. P. As the price falls to Rs. P1, the demand rises to Q1 units respectively. Thus

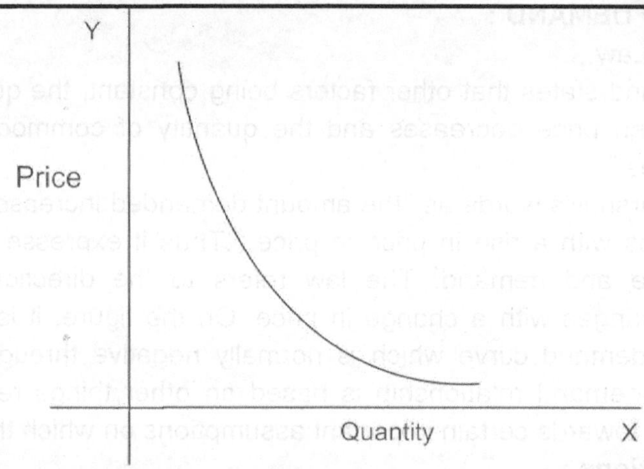

the demand curves DD, shows increase in demand of commodity when its price falls. This indicates the inverse relation between price and quantity demanded.

- **Causes of Downward Sloping Demand Curve**

Why does a demand curve slope downward from left to right? The reasons for this also clarify the working of the law of demand. The following are the main reasons for the downwards sloping demand curve.

1) **The law of demand is based on the law of Diminishing Marginal Utility.**

According to this law, when a consumer buys more units of a commodity, the marginal utility of that commodity continues to decline .Therefore, the consumer will buy more units will be high and the consumer will be prepared to pay more for the commodity. This proves that the demand will be more at a lower price and it will be less at a higher price. That is why the demand curve is downward sloping.

The law of diminishing marginal utility states that with an increase in the units of a commodity consumed, every additional unit of the commodity given lesser satisfaction to the consumer In other words, marginal utility of the commodity falls with an increase in its consumption. A consumer will maximize his satisfaction when he/she equalize the marginal utility of the commodity with its price i.e.,

$$\underline{MUx = Px}$$

If price increases and utility decreases consumer will not demand or decreases the demand of commodity.

2) **Real Income Effect:**

A change in price will change in real income of consumer. When price of commodity increases real income of consumer decreases so consumer decrease his demand of commodity.

Income	Price	Real income	Demand
500	100	400	4
500	200	300	3

In above example if income of consumer is 500 and to earn that income consumer spends 100 for petrol, so he receives 400 which is his real income. But when price of petrol increases to 100 and income of consumer remains constant real income decreases so consumer will decreases his demand. So when price increases, demand decreases because real income of consumer decreases.

3) **Substitution Effect:**

When price of commodity increases consumer can decrease his demand because for that commodity substitutes goods is available in market. E.g. if commodity A and commodity B is substitute goods and when price of A goods increases consume can switch to commodity B, therefore demand for A commodity decreases when its price increases.

Price effect = Real Income effect + Substitution Effect

According to above mention formula we can say that price effect brings two effects simultaneously that's real income effect and substitute effect. It means when price increases consumer's real income decreases so consumer switch to substitute goods.

4) **Number of consumer:**

If price of commodity is very less number of consumer can afford for demand for commodity. but when price of commodity decreases, commodity became affordable for large number of people therefore demand for such commodities increases.

e.g. If price of BMW car is 50,000,00, it will be demanded by less number of consumers and price of same decreases, it will be demanded by many consumers consumer.

➢ **Exceptions to Law of Demand :**

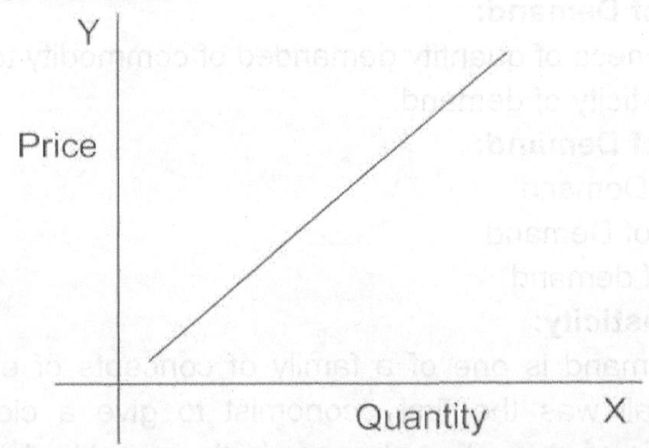

In certain cases, the demand curve slopes up from left to right, it has a positive slope. Under certain circumstances, consumers buy more when the price of a commodity rises and less when price falls, as shown by the *D* curve in Fig 8. Many causes are attributing to an upward sloping demand curve.

i) War :

If shortage is feared in anticipation of war of war, people may start buying for building stocks or for hoarding even when the price rises.

ii) Depression :

During a depression, the prizes of commodities are very low and the demand for them is also less. This is because of the lack of. Purchasing power with consumers.

iii) Giffen Paradox :

This concept is given by Sir Robert Giffen that's why thus known as Giffen paradox. If a commodity happens to be a necessity of life like wheat and it's price goes up, consumers are forced to curtail the consumption of more expensive foods like meat and fish, and wheat being still the cheapest food there will consume more of it. The marshallian example is applicable to developed Economies. In the case of an under developed economic with the fall in the price of an inferior commodity like maize, consumers will start consuming more of the superior commodity like wheat. As a result, the demand for maize will fall. This is what Marshall called the *giffen Paradox* which makes the demand curve to have a positive slope.

iv) Demonstration Effect :

If consumer are affected by the principal of conspicuous consumption or demonstration effect, there will to buy more of those commodities which confer distinction on the possessor, when their prices rise. On the other hand, with the fall in the prices of such articles, there demand falls, as is the case with diamonds

v) Ignorance Effect :

Consumer buy more at a higher price under the influence of the ignorance effect, where a commodity may be mistaken for some other commodity, due to deceptive packing, label.

3.4 Concept of Elasticity of Demand:

Meaning Elasticity of Demand:

Degree of responsiveness of quantity demanded of commodity to change in any factor of demand is called elasticity of demand.

Types of elasticity of Demand:

1. Price elasticity of Demand
2. Income elasticity of Demand
3. Cross Elasticity of demand

Meaning of price elasticity:

Price elasticity of demand is one of a family of concepts of elasticity. As pointed out above Alfred Marshall was the first economist to give a clear formulation of price elasticity. It is the ratio of proportion changes in the quantity demanded of a commodity to a given propitiation change in its price It is the ratio of a relation change in the quantity to a relative change in price.

$$PE = \frac{\%\text{change in quantity}}{\%\text{change in Price}}$$

➤ **Classification of price Elasticity of Demand**

Price elasticity of demand is generally classified under the following five sub-heads:

1) **Perfectly Elastic Demand :**

It refers to that situation where no change in price causes the change quantity demanded of the commodity, in this concept there will be no change in price but demand will change. The demand in such a case is hyper-sensitive and the elasticity of demand is infinite. It should, however, be remembered that cases of perfectly elastic demand are very rare in actual life and, as such only of theoretical interest.

Price	Demand
100	10
100	15

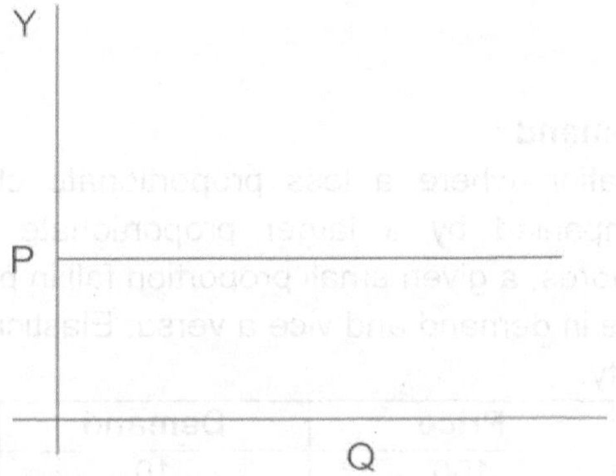

$$PE = \frac{\%\text{change in quantity}}{\%\text{change in Price}}$$

PE= infinity

In given schedule, price change by 0% but demand changes by 50%. Therefore demand is highly sensitive which will be perfectly elastic.

In given diagram, demand curve will be parallel to X axis because no change in price but quantity demand changes.

2) **Perfectly Inelastic Demand :**

It refers to that situation where changes in price, causes the demand remains unaffected. In other words, the price may change but the quantity demanded of the commodity remains unchanged. In this case elasticity of demand is zero. Perfectly Inelastic demand can be seen in market. It can be seen when the commodities are necessity e,g. salt.

Price	Demand
100	10
50	10

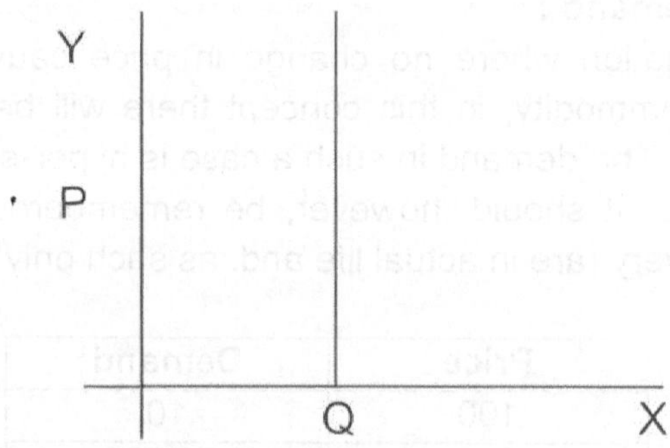

$$PE = \frac{\%\text{change in quantity}}{\%\text{change in Price}}$$

PE= 0

3) Relatively Elastic Demand :

It refers to that situation where a less proportionate change in the price of a commodity is accompanied by a larger proportionate changes in its quantity demanded. In other words, a given small proportion fall in price is followed by a large proportionate increase in demand and vice a versa. Elasticity of demand here is said to be greater than unity.

Price	Demand
100	10
80	15

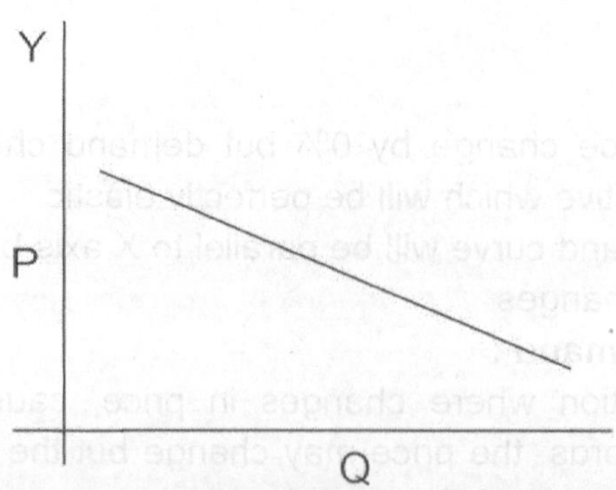

$$PE = \frac{\%change\ in\ quantity}{\%change\ in\ Price}$$

PE > 1

4) **Relatively Inelastic Demand :**

It refers to that situation where a big proportionate change in the price of commodity is accompanied by smaller proportionate change in its quantity demanded. In other words a given large proportionate fall in price is followed by a smaller proportionate increase in demand and vice versa. Elasticity of demand here is said to be less than unity.

Price	Demand
100	10
50	12

$$PE = \frac{\%change\ in\ quantity}{\%change\ in\ Price}$$

PE < 1

5) **Unitary Elastic Demand :**

It refers to that situation where a given propitiation changes in price is accompanied by an equally proportionate changes in the quantity demanded. In other words a given propitiation fall in price is followed by an equally proportionate fall in price is demanded and vice versa. Elasticity of demand here is said to be equal to unity .The curve in this case is referred to as **"rectangular hyperbola"** in technical language. It has a constant elasticity (or uniform elasticity) at every point.

Price	Demand
100	10
50	15

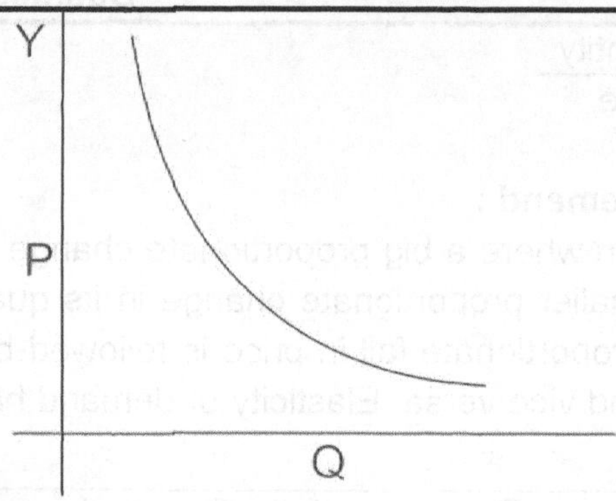

$$PE = \frac{\%\text{change in quantity}}{\%\text{change in Price}}$$

PE= 1

➢ **INCOME ELASTICITY OF DEMAND :**

Meaning :

Elasticity is a general concept; it can be used wherever there is a functional relationship between variables. Now we shift to what is called income elasticity of demand. Income elasticity of demand for a commodity shows the extent to which a consumer's demand for that commodity changes as a result of a change in his income. It shows the responsiveness of a consumer's purchases of that commodity to a change in his income. It can be defined as the ratio of proportionate change in the quantity demanded of the commodity to a given proportionate change in the income of the consumer. The income elasticity of demand can be measured by the application of the following formula:

$$\text{Income Elasticity} = \frac{\%\text{ change in the quantity demanded}}{\%\text{change in the income of the consumer}}$$

CLASSIFICATION OF INCOME ELASTICITY

Income elasticity of demand has generally a plus sign in front of it, though there can be other varieties of income elasticity as well. Like price elasticity, we can classify income elasticity under five heads.

1) **Zero Income Elasticity of Demand :**

This refers to the situation where a given increase in consumer's money-income does not result in any increase of the quantity demanded of the commodity. The quantity bought of the commodity remains constant despite the increase in the consumer's income. Symbolically, zero income elasticity of demand is expressed as it can be possible when commodities are inexpensive goods.

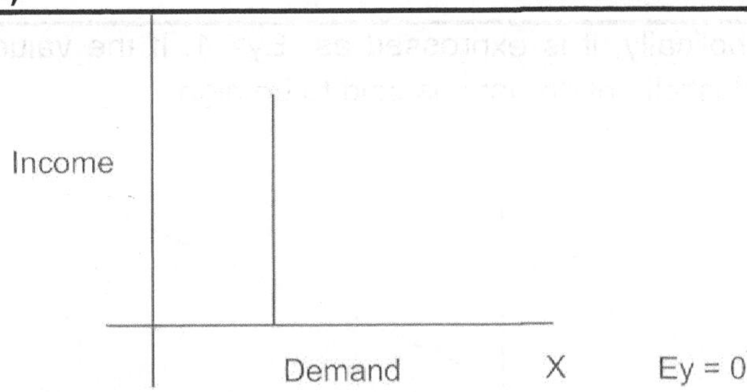

2) Negative Income Elasticity of Demand :

This refers to the situation where a given increase in the consumer's money-income is followed by an actual fall in the quantity demanded of the commodity. This happens in the case of economically inferior goods. Symbolically, negative income elasticity of demand is expressed as Ey< 0.

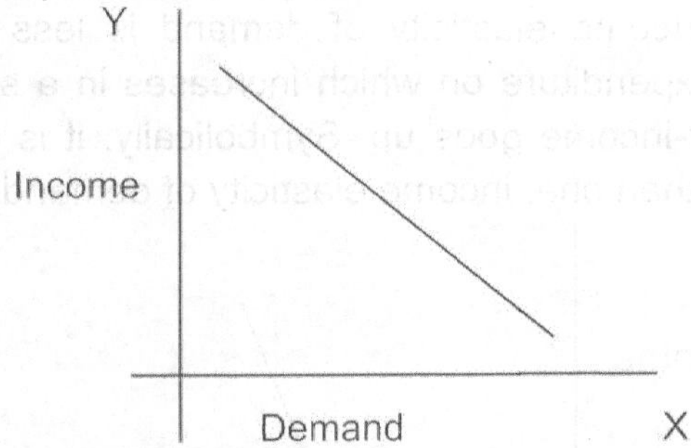

3) Unitary Income Elasticity of Demand :

This refers to the situation where the proportion of the consumer's income spent on the commodity in question, when he becomes richer and more prosperous. The income elasticity of demand here is equal to unity. Symbolically, unitary income elasticity of demand is expressed as Ey = 1

It can be possible when goods are Normal

Income

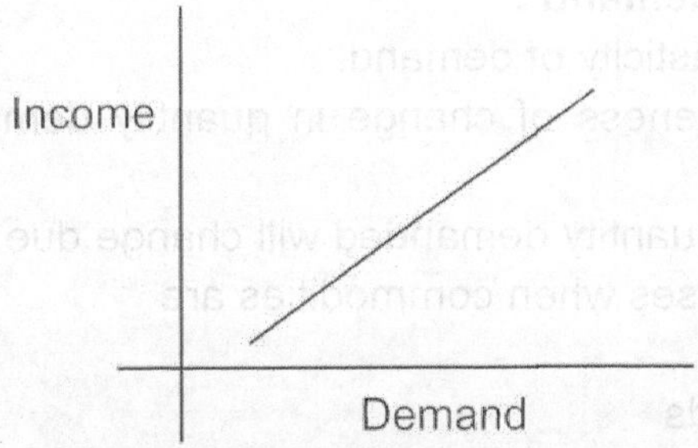

4) Income Elasticity of Demand Greater than Unity :

This refers to the situation where the consumer spends a greater proportion of his money-income on the commodity in question, when he becomes richer and more prosperous. The income elasticity of demand is greater than unity in the case of luxuries. Symbolically, it is expressed as Ey> 1. If the value of Ei is greater than one, income elasticity of demand is said to be high.

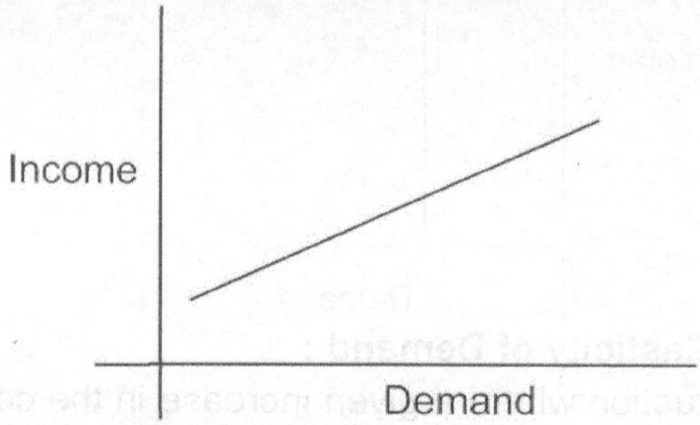

5) Income Elasticity of Demand Less than Unity :

This refers to the situation where the consumer spends a smaller proportion of his money-income on the commodity in question when he becomes richer and more prosperous. The income elasticity of demand is less than unity in the case of necessaries, the expenditure on which increases in a smaller proportion when the consumer's money-income goes up. Symbolically, it is expressed as Ey< 1, If the value of Ey is less than one, income elasticity of demand is said to be low.

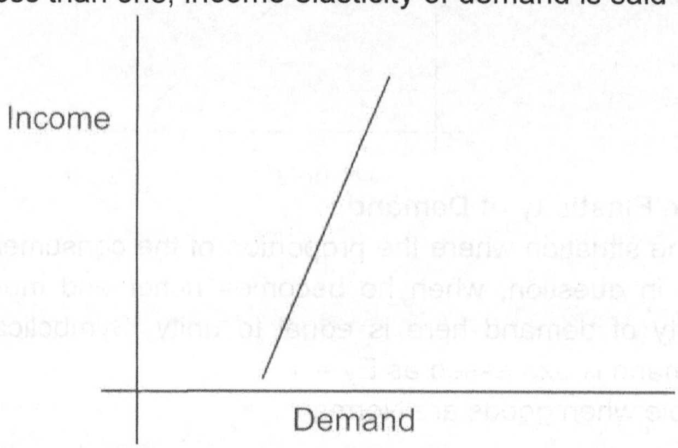

➢ **Cross elasticity of demand :**

Meaning of Cross elasticity of demand:

Degree of responsiveness of change in quantity demanded to change in price of related goods.

It means change in quantity demanded will change due price of related goods. It can be possible in two cases when commodities are

1) Substitute goods
2) Complementary goods

Types of Cross elastic demand

1) Positive cross elastic demand (substitute goods) :

When goods are substitute elasticity will be positive. Substitute good are those two or more goods can satisfy same need. So one of them only can be bought by consumer, e.g. Tea n Coffee. Such kinds of goods are also known as competitive goods. When good are substitute goods, Price of one commodity increases, demand of another commodity also increase. So there will be positive relation between price of one commodity and demand of its substitute goods.

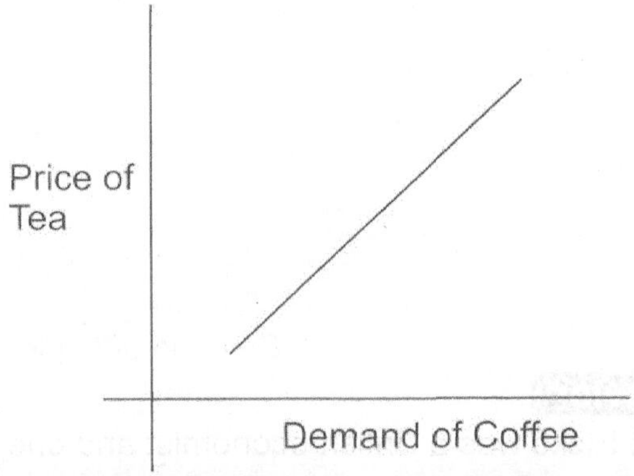

2) **Negative cross elastic demand (complimentary goods) :**

When goods are complimentary, elasticity will be negative. Complimentary goods are those two or more goods which will be bought simultaneously by the consumer because one of them will not satisfy need. E.g. Car n Petrol. When good are complimentary goods, Price of one commodity increases, demand of another commodity also decrease. So there will be negative relation between price of one commodity and demand of its complimentary goods.

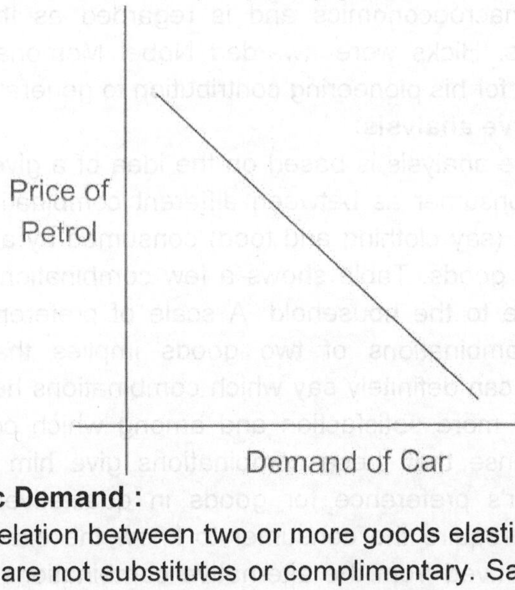

3) **Zero cross elastic Demand :**

When there is no relation between two or more goods elasticity will be zero. It means two of more good are not substitutes or complimentary. Say Book n Apple, price of one commodity will not make any effect on demand of another commodity. So cross elasticity will be zero.

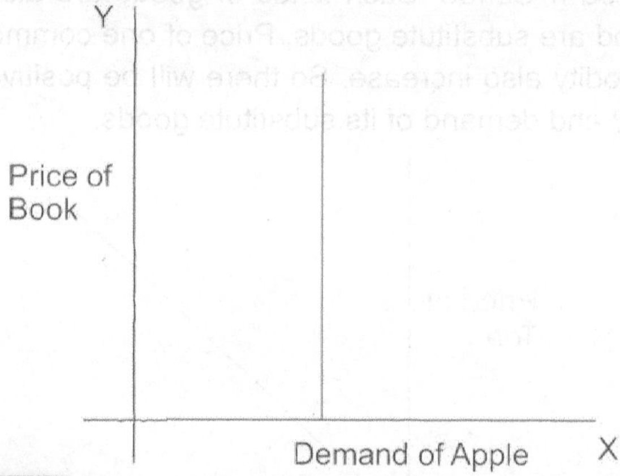

3.5 Consumer Behavior :

JR Hicks (1904-89) JR Hicks was a British economist and one of the most important and influential economists of the 20th century. He was among the generation of economists who contributed significantly to the development of various fields of economics. Among his various contributions in economics, the most familiar was in the theory of consumer demand. He is credited for having introduced the now-standard distinction between substitution effect and income effect in the demand theory. His other contributions in the field of economics were ordinal utility analysis, theory of wages, general equilibrium theory and welfare theory. Hicks developed the IS-LM model which gave an interaction of Keynesian view of macroeconomics and is regarded as the standard model of modern macroeconomics. Hicks were awarded Nobel Memorial Prize in Economics Sciences (jointly) in 1972 for his pioneering contribution to general equilibrium theory.

- **The indifference curve analysis:**

  The indifference curve analysis is based on the idea of a given scale of preference on the part of the consumer as between different combinations of two goods. An amount of two goods (say clothing and food) consumed by a household is called a combination of these goods. Table shows a few combinations (or bundles) of food and clothing available to the household. A scale of preference of a consumer as between different combinations of two goods implies that as between these combinations he/she can definitely say which combinations he/she prefers to others as they give him/her more satisfaction and among which combinations he/she is indifferent (in the sense that these combinations give him same satisfaction). It shows the consumer's preference for goods in qualitative terms. The scale of preference does not require the consumer to know the exact amount of utility (in quantitative terms) derived from the alternative combinations. All that is necessary for the consumer to know is which combinations give him same utility, and which combinations give him more or less utility.

➢ Indifference Curve

Indifference curve is combination of two commodities which gives equal level of satisfaction.

We start by developing a single indifference curve. To do this, we give our imaginary household some quantities of two goods-say clothing and food-which give him equal satisfaction. This is shown by an indifference schedule as illustrated in Table. An indifference schedule refers to a schedule that shows various combinations of two goods which give equal amount of satisfaction to the consumer. Since each of these combinations gives the household equal satisfaction, the household is indifferent among them.

Table of Indifference Schedule

Combination Food (units) Clothing (units) Marginal Rate of Substitution

Combination	Food	Clothing	MRS
A	1	10	-
B	2	7	1:3
C	3	5	1:2
D	4	4	1:1

The above schedule shows that the consumer gets equal satisfaction from all the four combinations, namely A, B, C and D, of food and clothing. At combination 'A', he has 1 unit of food and 10 units of clothing; in combination `B' he has 2 units of food and 7 units of clothing, and so on. In order to have one more unit of food, he/she has to give up some quantity of the clothing in such a way that there is no change in the level of his satisfaction from each of these combinations.

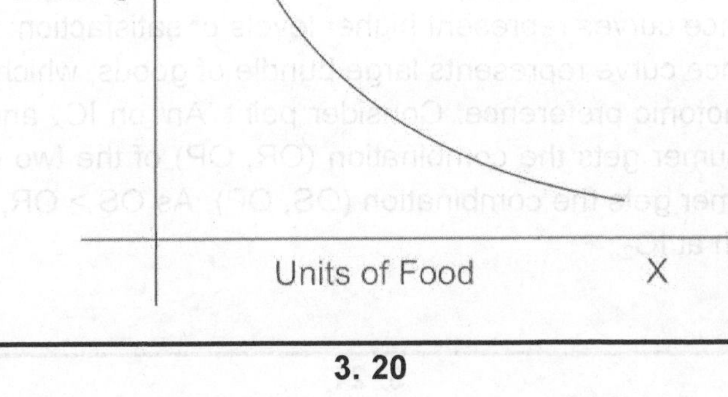

➢ **Properties of indifference curve**

1) Indifference curve slopes left to right downward :

A curve slope negatively as the units of food is increasing and units of clothing are decreasing. So while increasing units of one commodity, units of other commodity will be given up because consumer cannot buy both the commodity simultaneously as income of consumer is limited.

2) Indifference curve is convex in shape :

A curve is convex in shape because of MRS (Marginal rate of substitute) is decreasing. When consumer increases units of food he has to decreases some units of clothing, for 1 unit of food he decreases 3 units of clothing then again he will buy one more food but this he will give up 2 clothing. he will be not ready to give up 3 this time because marginal utility of 2nd food decreases.

➢ **MRS (Marginal rate if substitute) :**

Marginal rate if substitute is the rate which consumer is willing to substitute or replaces one goods with other goods.

➢ **Indifference Map :**

Indifference map is set of many indifference curve which gives different level of satisfaction.

Indifference Map : Goods

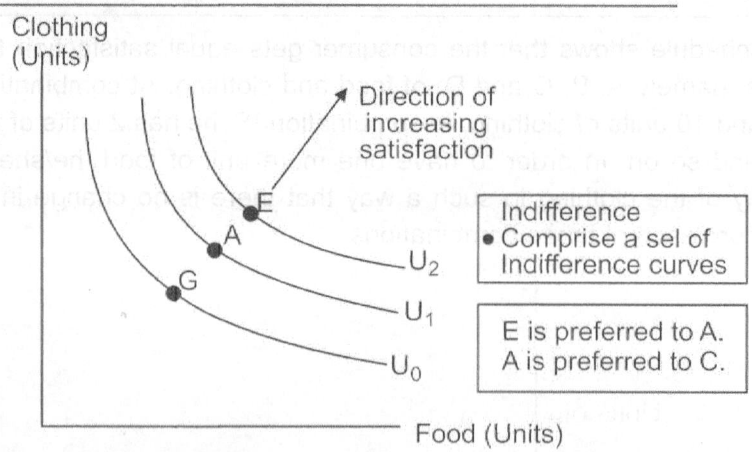

➢ **Properties of indifference map :**

Higher Indifference curves represent higher levels of satisfaction:

Higher indifference curve represents large bundle of goods, which means more utility because of monotonic preference. Consider point 'An' on IC_X and point 'B' on IC_2 in Fig. At 'A', consumer gets the combination (OR, OP) of the two commodities X and Y. At 'B', consumer gets the combination (OS, OP). As OS > OR, the consumer gets more satisfaction at IC_2.

4.Indifference curves can never intersect each other:

As two indifference curves cannot represent the same level of satisfaction, they cannot intersect each other. It means, only one indifference curve will pass through a given point on an indifference map. In Fig. satisfaction from point A and from B on IC_1 will be the same.

Similarly, points A and C on IC_2 also give the same level of satisfaction. It means, points B and C should also give the same level of satisfaction. However, this is not possible, as B and C lie on two different indifference curves, IC_1 and IC_2 respectively and represent different levels of satisfaction. Therefore, two indifference curves cannot intersect each other.

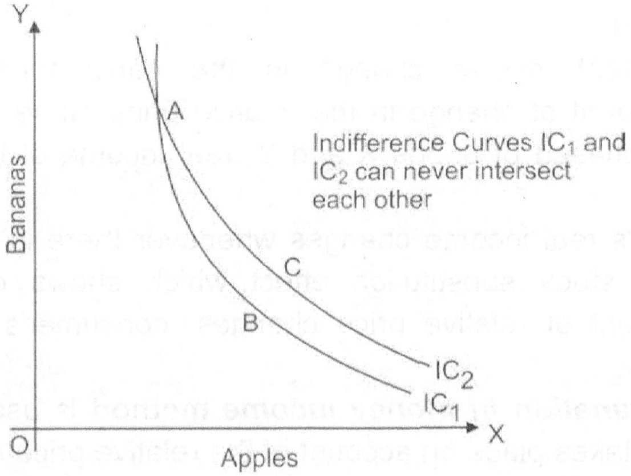

- A **price effect :**

  A **price effect** represents change in consumer's optimal consumption combination on account of change in the price of a good and thereby changes in its quantity purchased, price of another good and consumer's income remaining unchanged. The consumer is better-off when optimal consumption combination is located on a higher indifference curve and vice versa

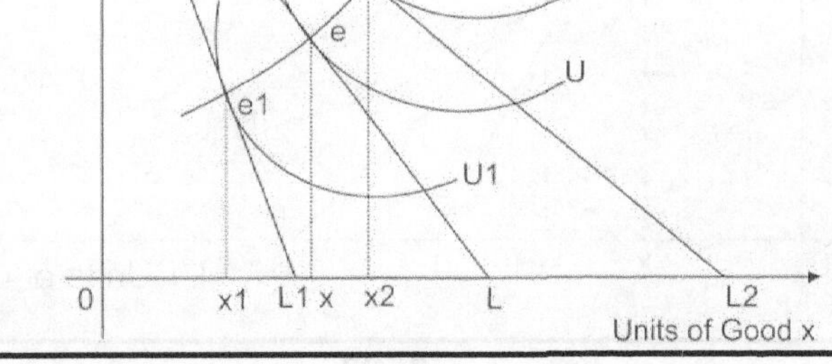

Impact of fall in price of good X on its quantity demanded		
Type of Price Effect	**Nature of Good X**	**Quantity Demanded of Good X**
Positive	Normal	↑
Negative	Inferior (including Giffen Goods)	↓
Zero	Neutral	No Change in Quantity Demanded

TYPE OF PRICE EFFECTS

A **substitution effect :**

a **substitution effect** shows change in the consumer's optimal consumption combination on account of change in the relative price alone and thereby changes in her/his quantity purchased of goods X and Y, real income of the consumer remaining unchanged.

Note that consumer's real income changes whenever there is a relative price change. Then, how do we study substitution effect which shows changes in consumer's purchases on account of relative price changes, consumer's real income remaining unchanged?

A *compensatory variation in money income* method is used to neutralize the real income change that takes place on account of the relative price change. The consumer's money income is sufficiently adjusted to compensate her/him for real income changes on account of change in the price of a good.

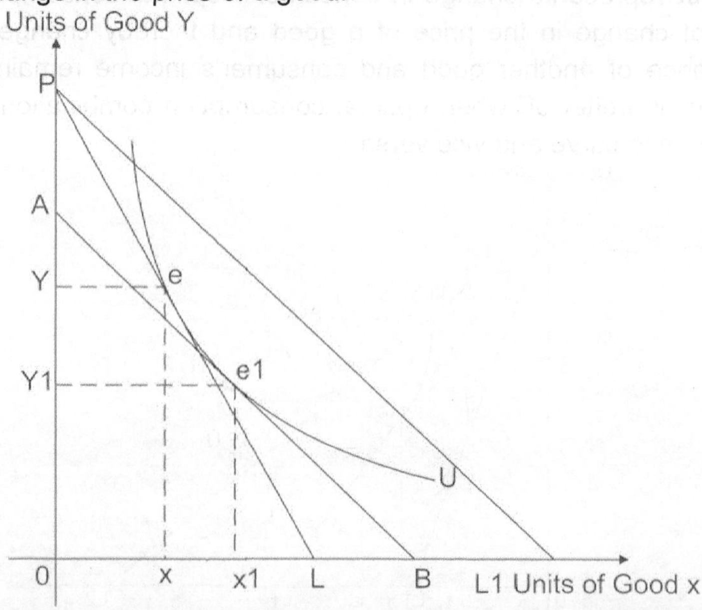

When the price of good X decreases, the budget constraint then becomes flatter, as the lower end point moves rightward. This is shown by budget constraint PL_1. The real income of the consumer also increases. This increase in real income will be neutralized through *Compensatory Variation in Money Income* so that the real income of the consumer remains unchanged. In other words we need to reduce consumer's money income to bring her/him at initial real income level. This adjustment in money income shifts the budget constraint backwards and it is a parallel shift as shown by the price line AB.

An income effect

An **income effect** represents change in consumer's optimal consumption combination on account of change in her/his income and thereby changes in her/his quantity purchased, prices of goods X (P_X) and Y (P_Y)remaining unchanged. The consumer is better-off when optimal consumption combination is located on a higher indifference curve and vice versa.

Understand that like price effect; a consumer's responses to income changes also differ depending upon the nature of the good, viz. a normal good, inferior good or a neutral good. These are summarized in chart.

TYPE OF INCOME EFFECTS

Impact of fall in rise in income on quantity demanded of good X		
Type of Income Effect	**Nature of Good X**	**Quantity Demanded of Good X**
Positive	Normal	↑
Negative	Inferior (including Giffen Goods)	↓
Zero	Neutral	No Change in Quantity Demanded

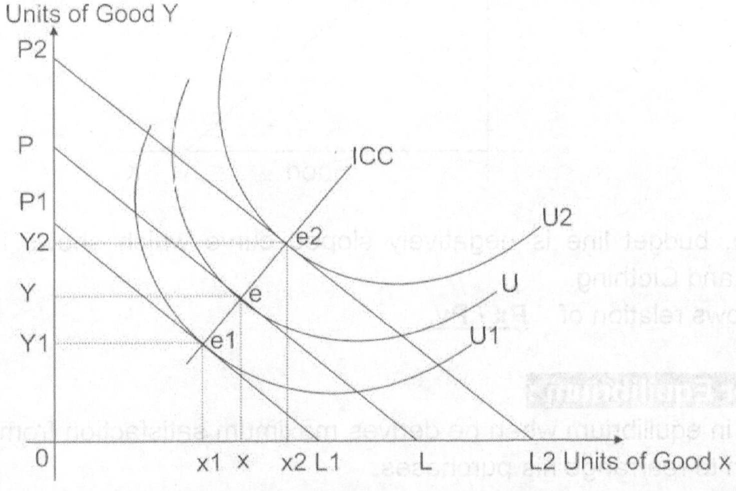

Whenever income of the consumer change, the entire budget constraint shifts outwards or inwards. With decrease in income the entire budget constraint shifts inwards and it is a parallel shift. Similarly, when income increases then entire budget constraint shifts outwards and it is a parallel shift. This is shown by budget constraint P_2L_2 in Figure.

➢ **Budget line :**

"A budget line shows different combination of two goods which can be purchased by consumer at given price and given income of the consumer. "

Clothing	Food	Total Expenditure
5	0	5 x 20 + 0 x 10 = 100
4	2	4 x 20 + 2 x 10 = 100
3	4	3 x 20 + 4 x 10 = 100
2	6	2 x 20 + 6 x 10 = 100
1	8	1 x 20 + 8 x 10 = 100
0	10	0 x 20 + 10 x 10 = 100

Price of Clothing = 20
Price of Food is = 10
Total income of consumer = 100

In given table consumer is increasing units of food by 2 but for this he has decreases 1 unit of clothing. Because price of clothing is double of price of Food. Even utility of money remains constant so every time consumer substitutes 2 foods for one clothing.

Budget Line Curve

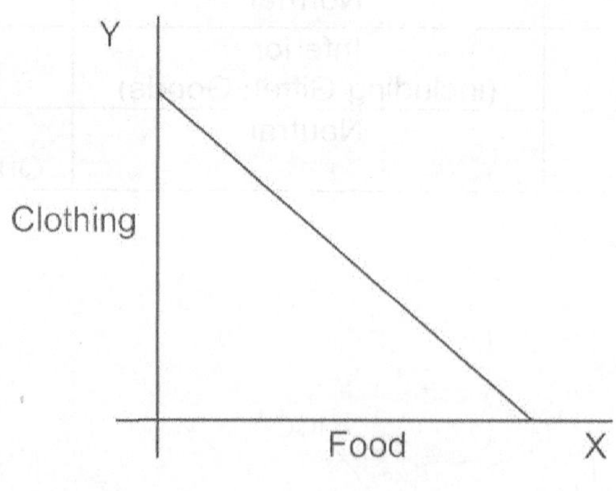

In given curve, budget line is negatively sloped curve which shows inverse relation between Food and Clothing.

Budget line shows relation of **Px / Py.**

3.6 Consumer Equilibrium :

A consumer is in equilibrium when he derives maximum satisfaction from the goods and is in no position to rearrange his purchases.

Assumptions :

- There is a defined indifference map showing the consumer's scale of preferences across different combinations of two goods X and Y.
- The consumer has a fixed money income and wants to spend it completely on the goods X and Y.
- The prices of the goods X and Y are fixed for the consumer.
- The goods are homogenous and divisible.
- The consumer acts rationally and maximizes his satisfaction.

Consumers Equilibrium :

In order to display the combination of two goods X and Y, that the consumer buys to be in equilibrium, let's bring his indifference curves and budget line together.

We know that,

- **Indifference Map :**
  Shows the consumer's preference scale between various combinations of two goods
- **Budget Line :**
  Depicts various combinations that he can afford to buy with his money income and prices of both the goods.
  In the following figure, we depict an indifference map with 5 indifference curves – IC_1, IC_2, IC_3, IC_4, and IC_5 along with the budget line PL for good X and good Y.

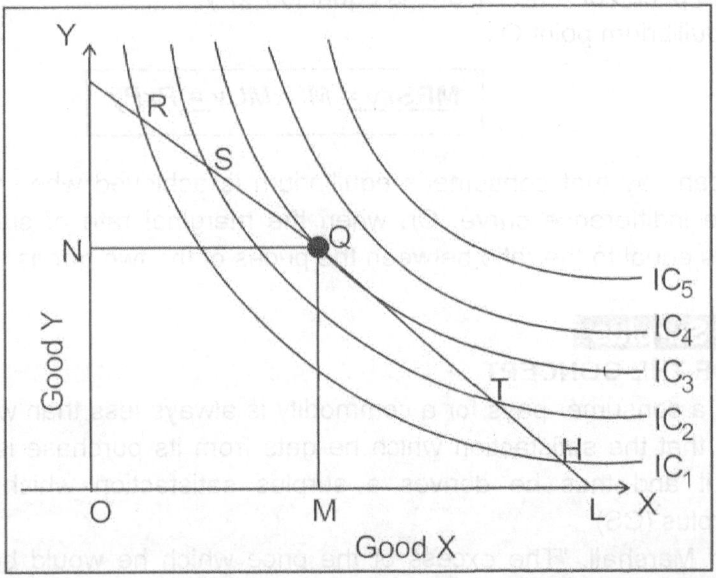

From the figure, we can see that the combinations R, S, Q, T, and H cost the same to the consumer. In order to maximize his level of satisfaction, the consumer will try to reach the highest indifference curve. Since we have assumed a budget constraint, he will be forced to remain on the budget line.

So, which combination will he choose?

Let's say that he chooses the combination R. From Fig. 1, we can see that R lies on a lower indifference curve – IC_1. He can easily afford the combinations S, Q, or T which lie on the higher ICs. Even if he chooses the combination H, the argument is similar since H lies on the curve IC_1 too.

Next, let's look at the combination S lying on the curve IC_2. Here again, he can reach a higher level of satisfaction within his budget by choosing the combination Q lying on IC_3 – higher indifference curve level. The argument is similar for the combination T since T lies on the curve IC_2 too.

Therefore, we are left with the combination Q.

What happens if he chooses the combination Q?

This is the best choice since Q lies on his budget line and pts puts him on the highest possible indifference curve, IC_3. While there are higher curves, IC_4 and IC_5, they are beyond his budget. Therefore, he reaches the equilibrium at point Q on curve IC_3.

Notice that at this point, the budget line PL is tangential to the indifference curve IC_3. Also, in this position, the consumer buys OM quantity of X and ON quantity of Y.

Since point Q is the tangent point, the slopes of line PL and curve IC_3 are equal at this point. Further, the slope of the indifference curve shows a marginal rate of substitution of X for Y (MRSxy) equal to *MUxMUy*. Also, the slope of the price line (PL) indicates the ratio between the prices of X and Y and is equal to *PxPy*.

Hence, at the equilibrium point Q,

MRSxy = *MUxMUy* = *PxPy*

Therefore, we can say that consumer's equilibrium is achieved when the price line is tangential to the indifference curve. Or, when the marginal rate of substitution of the goods X and Y is equal to the ratio between the prices of the two goods.

3.7 Consumer Surplus :

STATEMENT OF THE CONCEPT

The price which a consumer pays for a commodity is always less than what he is willing to pay for it, so that the satisfaction which he gets from its purchase is more than the price paid for it and thus he derives a surplus satisfaction which Marshall calls Consumer's Surplus (CS).

In the words of Marshall, "The excess of the price which he would be willing to pay rather than go without the thing, over that which he actually does pay, is the economic measure of the surplus satisfaction. It may be called "consumer's surplus." Instances of commodities from which we derive consumer's surplus in our daily life are salt, newspapers, postcard, matches, etc. Consumer's surplus, according to Marshall, is a part of the benefit which a person derives from his environment or conjuncture. To illustrate,

Quantity	Price	MU	Price / MU relation	Consumer status
1	500	700	MU > Price	Consumer Surplus
2	500	600	MU > Price	Consumer Surplus
3	500	500	MU = Price	Consumer Equilibrium
4	500	400	MU < Price	Consumer disequilibrium

Diagram of consumer surplus

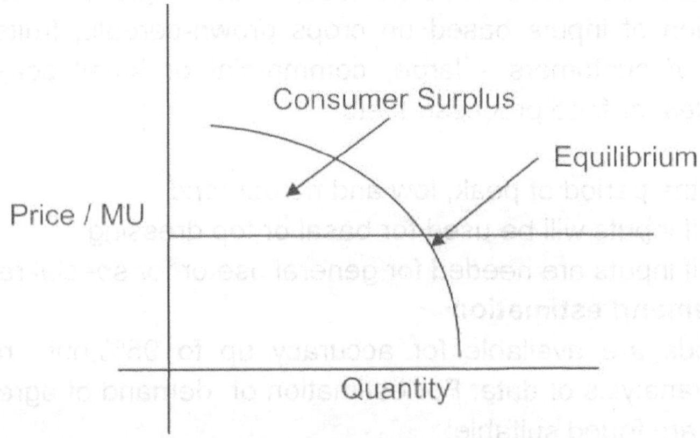

1) Where the MU is greater than price which consumer is ready to pay will be consumer surplus.

MU > Price

2) Where the MU is equal to price which consumer is ready to pay will be consumer Equilibrium.

MU = Price

3.8 Demand Estimation and Demand Forecasting Marketing and Objectives:

Demand estimation in managerial economics refers to predicting how consumers will behave in relation to your products and services in the future. The estimation is often based on a number of different variables that can include changes in price, changes in how your competition increases or decreases its prices, and economic factors such as a recession, which would affect consumer buying. By applying these variables, you can analyze how your customer's demands might change for the better or for the worse depending on a specific factor. As a result, you may decide that you can raise prices because demand will remain steady or even increase, or you may decide that you will have to pull back on production because circumstances are not likely to be favorable.

Demand estimation in managerial economics is an important way for you to determine the short-term and long-term course of your business

➢ Objectives of demand estimation

How much to sell

Fixing the product wise, crop wise, month wise, and year wise targets for sale of inputs. The targets may also be fixed for different types of fertilizers varieties of seeds and brands & types of CPP.

Where to sell Geographical area –

Identification of market area i.e. provinces, districts, group of villages etc Product range- determination of inputs based on crops grown-cereals, fruits or vegetables or live stock Profile of customers - large, commercial or small scale farmers. Export growers, wheat miles, or food processors etc

When to sell

- To determine the period of peak, low and no demand
- To determine if inputs will be used for basal or top dressing
- To determine if inputs are needed for general use or for special requirements

➢ **Methods of demand estimation**

Several methods are available for accuracy up to 95%,but require accurate collection and analysis of data; For estimation of demand of agree inputs, following three methods are found suitable;

1) Survey of buyers intention method
2) Composite sales staff opinion method
3) Expert opinion method

1) Survey of Buyer's Intentions Method :

- Relies on the information base of "what people say"
- Believes that buyers themselves are the best source of information
- A questionnaire is prepared asking how much inputs will farmer use next year.
- Questionnaire are posted to as many as possible farmers/opinion leaders

2) Sales staff Opinion Method :

Sales staff Opinion Method IS based on the belief that sales staff can provide correct estimates of their Sales territories IS appropriate when number of customers is large and spread out in wide locations.

3) Expert Opinion Method :

- Believes that experts, research agencies, advisors, consultants, opinion leaders and sales executives maintain useful information and area good source
- Information can be secured as per need at a short notice with less cost
- Is convenient for small enterprises
- Accuracy depends on the level of experts and can be up to 90%

  Info is collected from field and regional sales offices and consolidated at HQ

Demand forecasting :

Demand forecasting means an estimation of the level of demand that might be realized in future under given circumstances. These are concerned with the predictions of demand for products or services to minimize the uncertainties of the unknown future. These forecasts on demand facilitate in formulating material and capacity plans and serves as inputs to financial, marketing and personnel planning. The demand forecast itself may be generated in a number of ways, many of which depend heavily upon sales and marketing information.

The objectives of demand forecasting are different in case of short run and long run forecasts.

Short Run Forecasting

Short run forecasting is usually a period not exceeding one year. The following are the objectives of short run demand forecasting.

- To evolve a suitable production policy: Short term forecasts help the firm to plan the production so as to avoid the problems of over production and short supply.
- To plan the purchase pf raw materials: The firm's can plan the purchase of raw materials at appropriate time to reduce the cost and control inventories.
- To plan short term financial requirements: The firms require not only short term funds for purchase of raw materials and payment of wages, but also medium term funds for replacement and renewal to maintain productive efficiency.
- To determine appropriate price policy: Short run forecasting helps the firm to evolve a suitable price policy depending upon the expected market conditions to maintain consistent sales.
- To fix sales targets: Realistic sales targets can be fixed for the salesmen on the basis of short term demand forecasting. If the targets are too high the salesmen may fail to achieve them and they will get discouraged. If the targets are too low the salesmen will achieve the targets so easily that the incentives will prove meaningless.

Long Run Forecasting :

Long run forecasting is generally for a period exceeding 3 years. The following are the objectives of long run demand forecasting.

- To plan the establishment of a new unit or expansion of an existing unit: Planning of a new unit or expansion of an existing unit requires an analysis of the long term demand potential of the products. The competitive strength of the firm will be greater if it has better knowledge than the rivals of the growth trends in the economy.
- To plan long term financial requirements: Long run forecasts are essential to assess long term financial requirements. When the funds required for expansion, modernization and diversification are large, it takes time to make necessary arrangements for raising sufficient resources through long term loans and the issue of shares and debentures.

- To plan manpower requirements: Long term demand forecasting is useful for manpower planning. Training and personnel development can be started well in advance on the basis of estimates of manpower requirements assessed according to long term demand forecasts.

The Basics :

Demand estimation is a prediction focusing on future consumer behavior. It predicts demand for a business's products or services by applying a set of variables that show how, for example, price changes, a competitor's pricing strategy or changes in consumer income levels will affect product demand. Once armed with this information, management can then begin to make strategic business decisions ranging from reviewing pricing strategies to setting product inventory levels to deciding whether to make fixed asset investments and whether to introduce a new product or enter a new market.

Survey Method :

Consumer interviews, surveys and focus group meetings are a grass-roots method of estimating demand. The method operates under the idea that consumers know themselves best and that interacting with consumers directly is the best way to estimate future product demand. Getting information directly from consumers, however, decreases objectivity and increases the chance of errors. It can be difficult, for example, to get a truly random sample of the target consumer population. Consumer responses may also be biased in that responses may not reflect what a consumer will do, but rather what they would like to do, or a consumer may be unable to provide a precise or accurate response.

Market Study Method :

Market studies are a direct demand estimation method that combines consumer interaction with science. The process starts by setting a constant, such as price, and variables such as size and/or color. Market studies then display products at, for example, the same price, but in a variety of sizes and locations or settings over a period of time. Once the study is complete, analyzing the results reveals how demand for the product at that price changes according to, in this case, size or color.

Regression Analysis Method :

Demand estimation can also rely on regression analysis, a statistical way to find the best relationship between a dependent variable – in this case, product demand – and one or more independent variables, such as price or location. Although fully understanding demand estimation calculations requires a background in statistics, the process is not difficult to understand. Setup starts by identifying and obtaining data, such as cross-sectional market data or results of a time study or consumer survey on the independent variable or variables to be used in the calculation. Next comes choosing between using a simple or multiple regression model, depending on whether the calculation includes one or multiple variables. Both models display demand as an unknown. Parameters such as a specific price or average annual income are set. Statistical calculations can then begin, and management can move on to interpreting results.

Points to be remember

1) **Meaning of utility :**

Utility denotes satisfaction. It refers how consumer ranks different goods and services.

2) **THE CARDINAL AND ORDINAL UTILITY APPROACH :**

The cardinal or neo–classical utility analysis refers to the theory of consumer demand as built by Marshal, Pigou and others. This theory is based on the cordial measurement of utility which assumes that utility is measurable in numerical form and addictive.

3) **Meaning of Ordinal utility :**

The **Ordinal Utility** is based on the fact that the utility of a commodity cannot be measured in numerical term, but however, it can be proved that utility derived from commodity may be more, less or equal by comparing two or more commodities. This concept is given by J R Hicks and Allen.

4) **Utility derived from all the units of commodity is called total utility.**

$$\textbf{Total Utility} = MU_1 + MU_2 + MU_3 \ldots\ldots + MU_{nth}$$

5) **Marginal utility :**

Utility derived from every additional unit of commodity is called marginal utility.

$$\textbf{Marginal Utility} = TU_n - TU_{n-}$$

6) **LAW OF DIMINISHING MARGINAL UTILITY :**

"The law states that as the consumer consumes units of commodity one by one, utility derived from every additional unit i.e. marginal utility decreases."

7) **MEANING OF DEMAND :**

The demand for a commodity is its quantity which consumers are willing and able to buy at various prices during a given period of time.

8) **Demand Functions**

The demand functions are an algebraic expression of the relationship between demand for a community and its various determinants that affect this quantity.

9) THE LAW OF DEMAND :

"Law of demand states that other factors being constant, the quantity of commodity increases when price decreases and the quantity of commodity decreases when price increases."

10) Concept of Elasticity of Demand :

Elasticity of Demand

Degree of responsiveness of quantity demanded of commodity to change in any factor of demand is called elasticity of demand.

Types of elasticity of Demand

a) Price elasticity of Demand
b) Income elasticity of Demand
c) Cross Elasticity of demand

11) Consumer Behavior

The indifference curve analysis

The indifference curve analysis is based on the idea of a given scale of preference on the part of the consumer as between different combinations of two goods

Indifference Curve

Indifference curve is combination of two commodities which gives equal level of satisfaction.

12) MRS (Marginal rate if substitute) :

Marginal rate if substitute is the rate which consumer is willing to substitute or replaces one goods with other goods.

13) Indifference Map :

Indifference map is set of many indifference curve which gives different level of satisfaction.

14) Budget line :

"A budget line shows different combination of two goods which can be purchased by consumer at given price and

15) Consumers Equilibrium :

A consumer is in equilibrium when he derives maximum satisfaction from the goods and is in no position to rearrange his purchases.

MRSxy = MUxMUy = PxPy

16) The Concept of Consumer's Surplus

MUx > Px

17) Demand Estimation :

Demand estimation in managerial economics refers to predicting how consumers will behave in relation to your products and services in the future.

18) Methods of demand estimation :

a) Survey of buyers intention method

b) Composite sales staff opinion method

c) Expert opinion method

19) Demand forecasting :

Demand forecasting means an estimation of the level of demand that might be realized in future under given circumstances.

Questions for discussion

❖ **Write the answers in details of following question.**

1) Explain the concept of cardinal and ordinal utility in details.
2) Explain marginal and total utility, relation between MU and TU.
3) What is law diminishing marginal utility?
4) What is demand function ?
5) Explain law of demand.
6) What are exceptions of law of demand?
7) What are types of elasticity?
8) What are the types of price elasticity?
9) Explain the types of income elasticity?
10) What is cross elasticity?
11) Explain indifference curve with its features in details.
12) Explain indifference map with its features in details.
13) What are the income, price and substitute effects in indifference curve?
14) What is budget line?
15) Explain consumer equilibrium by using indifference curve.
16) What is consumer surplus?
17) What is demand Estimation?
18) What are the methods of demand Estimation?
19) What is demand Forecasting?
20) What the methods are of demand Forecasting?

PRODUCTION AND COST ANALYSIS

UNIT 4

4.1 Supply – Law of Supply:

Meaning of Supply

"A certain Quantity of Commodity which the producer is willing to sell at a particular price and particular period of time."

Three important aspects of supply which need to be noted in this definition of supply

1. Supply is a desired quantity ,i.e. how much producers are willing to sell and not how much they actually sell.
2. The second thing to note about supply is that supply is always expressed with reference to some price
3. Like demand, supply is a flow variable . Therefore, supply refers to the amount which producers or sellers are willing to sell in during a specific period of time-per day, per week, per month or per year.

LAW OF SUPPLY:

The law of supply states that, other things remaining the same. ,the quantity of any commodity that firms will produce and offer for sale rises with a rise in its price and falls with a fall in its price.

Individual SUPPLY Schedule

Price	Supply
100	10
200	20
300	30

An INDIVIDUAL supply schedule is a tabular presentation of the law of supply. It shows various quantity supply of commodity which single producer is willing to sell at various level of price in during a specific period of time.

- **INDIVIDUAL SUPPLY CURVE**

  An individual supply curve is defined as the curve which shows various quantities of a given commodity which an individual producer is willing to supply at different prices during a given period of time assuming no change in all other factors excepts the own price affecting supply of the commodity.

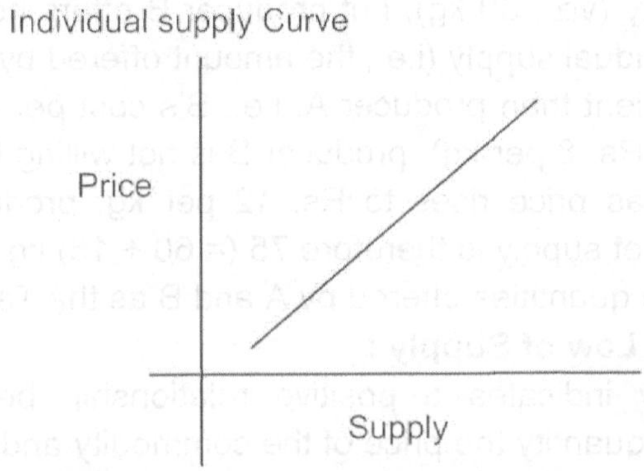

- **MARKET SUPPLY CURVE :**

  Market supply curve is the curve which shows various quantities of a commodity which all the products are willing to produce and at different prices during a given period of time, assuming that factors other than the own price of the good are given.

  Derivation of market supply

Price (Rs. Per kg)	Quantities Supplied		
	Producer A (kg per month)	Producer B (kg Per month)	Market Supply (kg per month) (ii + iii)
(i)	(ii)	(iii)	(iv)
4	0	0	0
8	30	0	30
12	60	15	75
16	90	30	120
20	120	45	165

Table : Individual and Market Supply Schedules

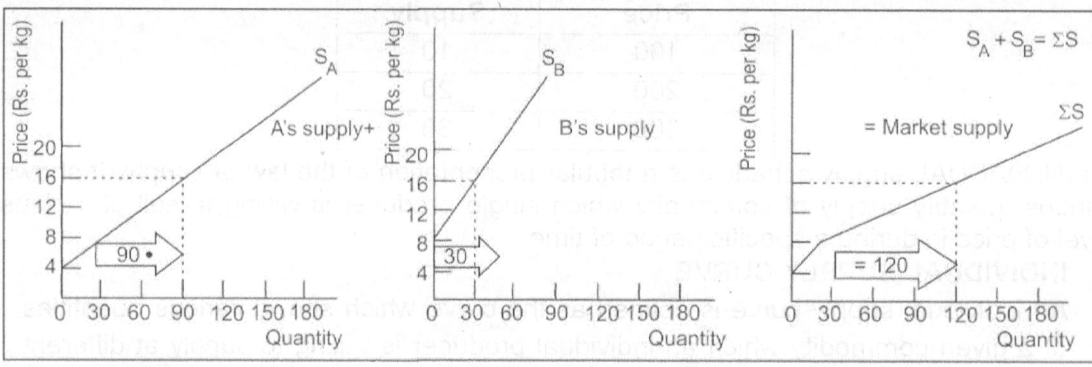

The market supply is derived simply by adding the quantities supplied at each price by the two producers. Thus, we see that when the market price of X is Rs. 8, producer A offers a positive quantity (viz., 30 kg), but producer B offers nothing. So, market supply is the same as the individual supply (i.e., the amount offered by producer A).

Producer B is less efficient than producer A, i.e., B's cost per unit is higher than that of A. So at this low price (Rs. 8 per kg), producer B is not willing to offer good X for sale in the market. However, as price rises to Rs. 12 per kg, producer A offers 60 kg and producer B 15 kg. Market supply is therefore 75 (= 60 + 15) kg. At each price the market supply is the sum of the quantities offered by A and B as the Table 4.4 indicates.

- **Explanation of the Law of Supply :**

  The law of supply indicates a positive relationship between the price of the commodity and the quantity the price of the commodity and the quantity supplied it is indicated by a positively sloping supply curve. positive slop of a supply curve can be explained in terms of three factors.

1) First reason is that the level of price determines the amount of profits. The higher the price of the commodity, the larger is the profit that can be ceteris paribus.
2) The positive slope of the supply curve also caused by the rise in the margin cost of production.
3) A rise in price would give incentive not only to the existing producers of a commodity, but it would also motivate the other prospective producers to produce this commodity

- **Exceptions to the Law of Supply :**

  The law of supply states that other things being equal, the supply of a commodity increases with a rise in price and decreases with a fall in price. There are however a few exceptions to the law of supply.

  1) **Need of cash :**

     If the producer needs of hard cash, he may sell his product at a price which may even be below the market price. So even at low price supply will be more.

2) Perishable goods :

In case of perishable production, supply of goods will remain constant because seller can no wait to increases in price so any level of price supply will remain constant.

3) Backward sloping supply curve of labor :

The increases in the price of a good or service sometimes leads to a decrease in its supply. In this case we can say if a higher wage rate given to labor, he will supply more labor but after certain level he will not increases his labor even at higher wage rate because he not a machine, he can feel tired. So supply curve bends backward.

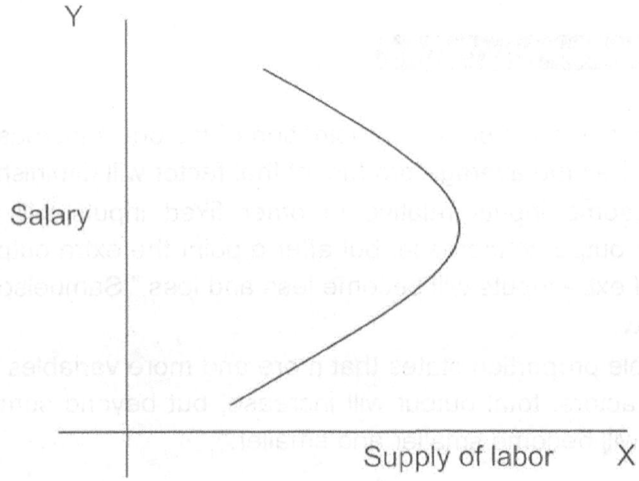

4.2 Production Function:

Production function (showing the input combinations that the firm can use to produce various levels of output) and the price of inputs, we can derive the firm's cost functions. These functions show the minimum costs that the firm would incur in producing various levels of output. For simplicity, we assume that the firm is too small to affect the prices of the inputs it uses. Thus, the prices of inputs remain constant regardless of the quantity demanded by the firm. In economics, costs include explicit and implicit costs.

Explicit costs :

Explicit costs are the actual out-of-pocket expenditures of the firm to purchase or hire the inputs it requires in production. These expenditures include the wages to hire labor, interest on borrowed capital, rent on land and buildings, and the expenditures on raw and semi finished materials.

Implicit costs :

Implicit costs refer to the value of the inputs owned and used by the firm in its own production processes. The value of these owned inputs must be imputed or estimated from what these inputs could earn in their best alternative use.

Definitions:

"The production function is a technical or engineering relation between input and output. As long as the natural laws of technology remain unchanged, the production function remains unchanged." Prof. L.R. Klein

Q = f (L, C, N)

Where Q = Quantity of output

L = Labor

C = Capital

N = Land

4.3 Law of Variable Proportions:

Definitions:

"As the proportion of the factor in a combination of factors is increased after a point, first the marginal and then the average product of that factor will diminish." Benham

"An increase in some inputs relative to other fixed inputs will in a given state of technology cause output to increase, but after a point the extra output resulting from the same additions of extra inputs will become less and less." Samuelson

Statement of Law:

"The law of variable proportion states that more and more variables increases with given amount of fixed factors, total output will increase, but beyond some point the resulting output increases will become smaller and smaller."

Assumptions:

Law of variable proportions is based on following assumptions:

i) **Constant Technology:**
   The state of technology is assumed to be given and constant. If there is an improvement in technology the production function will move upward.

ii) **Factor Proportions are Variable:**
   The law assumes that factor proportions are variable. If factors of production are to be combined in a fixed proportion, the law has no validity.

iii) **Homogeneous Factor Units:**
   The units of variable factor are homogeneous. Each unit is identical in quality and amount with every other unit.

Statement of the Law:

In order to understand the law of variable proportions we take the example of agriculture. Suppose land and labour are the only two factors of production.

➢ **Explanation of law :**
   In given schedule there are three types of production

Total production :

Amount of production produced by producer after using all the factors e.g. variables factors and fixed factors in given time period

Average production :

Output of per unit variable factor is called average production.

Average production = TP /L

Marginal Production :

Amount of production derived from every additional unit of variable factor is called marginal production.

Or

Change in total production due to addition of one more labor is called marginal production.

Marginal production = TP n – TP n-1

By keeping land as a fixed factor, the production of variable factor i.e., labour can be shown with the help of the following table:

Units of Land	Units of Labour	Total Production	Average Production	Marginal Production	
10 Acres	0	-	-	-	
"	1	20	20	20	
"	2	50	25	30	1st stage
"	3	90	30	40	MP > AP
"	4	120	30	30	AP = MP
"	5	140	28	20	
"	6	150	25	10	2nd stage
"	7	150	21.3	0	MP=0 and TP = maximum
"	8	140	17.5	-10	3rd stage MP < 0

From the table 1 it is clear that there are three stages of the law of variable proportion. In the first stage average production increases as there are more and more doses of labour and capital employed with fixed factors (land). We see that total product, average product, and marginal product increases but average product and marginal product increases up to 40 units. Later on, both start decreasing because proportion of workers to land was sufficient and land is not properly used. This is the end of the first stage.

The second stage starts from where the first stage ends or where AP=MP. In this stage, average product and marginal product start falling. We should note that marginal product falls at a faster rate than the average product. Here, total product increases at a diminishing rate. It is also maximum at 70 units of labour where marginal product becomes zero while average product is never zero or negative.

The third stage begins where second stage ends. This starts from 8th unit. Here, marginal product is negative and total product falls but average product is still positive. At this stage, any additional dose leads to positive nuisance because additional dose leads to negative marginal product.

Graphic Presentation:

In fig. 1, on OX axis, we have measured number of labourers while quantity of product is shown on OY axis. TP is total product curve. Up to point 'E', total product is increasing at increasing rate. Between points E and G it is increasing at the decreasing rate. Here marginal product has started falling. At point 'G' i.e., when 7 units of labourers are employed, total product is maximum while, marginal product is zero. Thereafter, it begins to diminish corresponding to negative marginal product. In the lower part of the figure MP is marginal product curve.

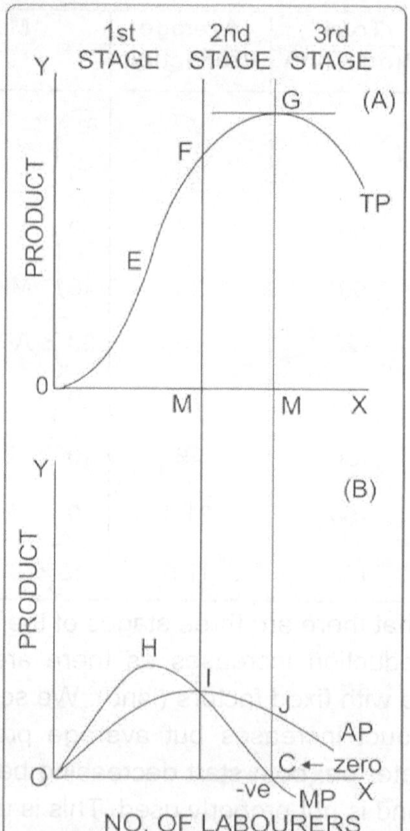

Up to point 'H' marginal product increases. At point 'H', i.e., when 3 units of labourers are employed, it is maximum. After that, marginal product begins to decrease. Before point 'I' marginal product becomes zero at point C and it turns negative. AP curve represents average product. Before point 'I', average product is less than marginal product. At point 'I' average product is maximum. Up to point T, average product increases but after that it starts to diminish.

Three Stages of the Law:

1) First Stage:

First stage starts from point 'O' and ends up to point F. At point F average product is maximum and is equal to marginal product. In this stage, total product increases initially at increasing rate up to point E. between 'E' and 'F' it increases at diminishing rate. Similarly marginal product also increases initially and reaches its maximum at point 'H'. Later on, it begins to diminish and becomes equal to average product at point T. In this stage, marginal product exceeds average product (MP > AP).

Causes of increasing Returns :

i) The main reason for increasing returns in the first stage is that in beginning the fixed factors are larger in quantity than the variable factor. when more units of the variable factor are applied to a fixed factor, the fixed factor is used more intensively and production increases rapidly.

ii) In the beginning, the fixed factor cannot be put to the due to the non-applicability of sufficient units of the variable factor. But the units of the variable factor are applied in sufficient quantities, division of labor and specialization lead to per unit increase in production and the law increasing returns operates.

iii) Another reason for increasing returns is that the fixed factors are indivisible which means that they must be used in a fixed minimum size. When more units of the variable factor are applied on such a fixed factor, production increases more than proportionately. These points towards the law of increasing returns.

2) Second Stage:

It begins from the point F. In this stage, total product increases at diminishing rate and is at its maximum at point 'G' correspondingly marginal product diminishes rapidly and becomes 'zero' at point 'C'. Average product is maximum at point 'I' and thereafter it begins to decrease. In this stage, marginal product is less than average product (MP < AP).

Reasons to diminishing returns :

But the law of diminishing Returns is not applicable to agriculture alone. Rather, it is of universal applicability. It is called the law in its general form, which states that if the proportion in which the factors of production are combined, is disturbed the average and marginal product of that factor will diminish. The distortion in the combination of factors may be either due to the scarcity of one in relation to other factors, In either case, diseconomies of production set in which raise costs and reduce output. For instance if plant is expanded by installing more machines, it may become unwieldy. Enterpreneneurial control and supervision become lax, and diminishing returns set in or there may arise scarcity of trained labour or raw material that leads to diminution in output.

In fact, it is the scarcity of one factor in relation to other factors which is the root cause of the law of diminishing returns. The element of Scarcity is found in factors because they cannot be substituted for one another. Mrs Joan Robinson explains it thus:

"What the law of diminishing Returns really states is that there is a limit to the extent to which one factor of production can be substituted for another or in other words that the elasticity of substitution between factors is not infinite". Suppose there is scarcity of jute, since no other fibre can be substituted for it perfectly, costs will rise with production, and diminishing Returns will operate. This is because jute is not in perfectly elastic supply to the industry. If the scarce factors is rigidly fixed and it cannot be substistuedby any other factors at all, Diminishing returns will at once set in if in a factory operated by electric power there being no other substitute for it frequent power breakdowns occur as is commonly the case in India. Production will fall and costs will rise in proportion as fixed costs will continue to be incurred even if the factory works for less hours than before.

3) **Third Stage:**

This stage begins beyond point 'G'. Here total product starts diminishing. Average product also declines. Marginal product turns negative. Law of diminishing returns firmly manifests itself. In this stage, no firm will produce anything. This happens because marginal product of the labour becomes negative. The employer will suffer losses by employing more units of labourers. However, of the three stages, a firm will like to produce up to any given point in the second stage only.

Total Product	**Marginal Product**	**Average Product**
Stage : I First increases at increasing rate then at diminishing rate.	Increases in the beginning then reaches a maximum and begins to decrease.	First increases, continues to increase and becomes maximum
Stage : II Continues to increase at diminishing rate and becomes maximum	Continues to diminish and becomes equal to zero.	Becomes equal to MP and then begins to diminish.
Stage : III Diminishes	Becomes negative	Continues to diminish but will always be greater than zero

In Which Stage Rational Decision is Possible:

To make the things simple, let us suppose that, as is variable factor and b is the fixed factor. And a1, a2 , a3....are units of a and b1 b2b3...... are unit of b.

Stage I is characterized by increasing AP, so that the total product must also be increasing. This means that the efficiency of the variable factor of production is increasing i.e., output per unit of a is increasing. The efficiency of b, the fixed factor, is also increasing, since the total product with b1 is increasing.

4.4 The law of Returns to Scale

The law of returns to scale describes the relationship between outputs and scale of inputs in the long-run when all the inputs are increased in the same proportion. In other words of Prof. Roger Miller, "Returns to scale refer to the relationship between changes in output and proportionate changes in all the factors of production." To meet a long-run change in demand, the firm increases its scale of production by using more space, more machines and laborers in the factory.

ASSUMPTIONS

This law assumes that

1) All factors (inputs) are variable but enterprise is fixed.

2) A worker works with given tools and implement.

3) Technological changes are absent.

4) There is perfect competition.

5) The product is measured in quantities.

EXPLANATION

Given these assumptions, when all inputs are increased in unchanged proportions and the scale of production is expanded, the effect on output shows three stages: increasing returns to scale, constant returns to scale and diminishing returns to scale. They are explained with the help of Table 2and Fig.5.

Returns to Scale in Physical Units

Unit	*Scale of Production*	*Total Returns*	*Marginal Returns*
1	1 Worker+ 2 Acres Land	8	8
2	2 Workers+ 4 Acres Land	17	9
3	3 Workers+ 6 Acres Land	27	10
4	4 Workers+ 8 Acres Land	38	11
5	5 Workers+ 10 Acres Land	49	11
6	6 Workers+ 12 Acres Land	59	10
7	7 Workers+ 14 Acres Land	68	9
8	8 Workers+ 16 Acres Land	76	8

1) Increasing Returns to Scale

Returns to scale increase because the increase in total output is more than proportional to the increase in all inputs.

The table reveals that in the beginning with the scale of production of (1 worker + 2 acres of land), total output is 8. To increase output when the scale of production is doubled (2 workers + 4 acres of land), total returns are more than doubled. They become 17. Now if the scale is trebled (3 workers + 6 acres of land), returns become more than three-fold, i.e., 27 it shows increasing returns to scale. In the figure RS is the return to scale curve where R and C portion indicates increasing returns.

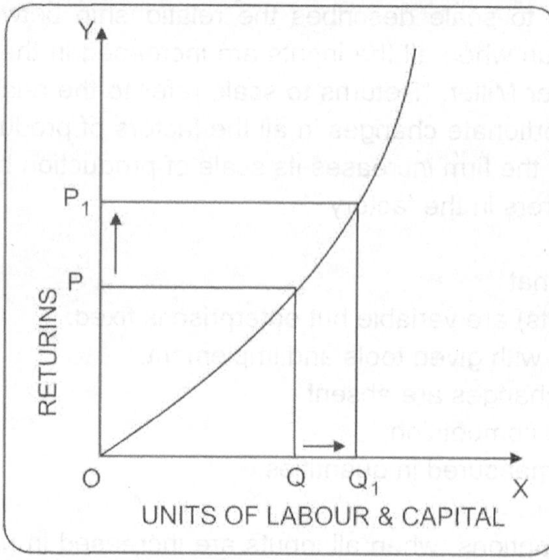

Causes of Increasing Returns to Scale

Returns to scale increase due to the following reasons:

i) Indivisibility of Factors:

Returns to scale increase because of the indivisibility of the factors of production. Indivisibility means that machines, management, labour, finance, etc, cannot be available in very small sizes. They are available only in certain small sizes. When a business unit expands, the returns to scale increase because the indivisible factors are employed to their maximum capacity.

ii) Specialisation and Division of Labour:

Increasing returns to scale also result from specialisation and division of labour. When the scale of the firm is expanded there is wide scope of specialisation and division of labour. Work can be divided into small tasks and workers can be concentrated to narrower range of processes. For this, specialized equipment can be installed. Thus with specialisation, efficiency increases and increasing returns to scale follow.

iii) Internal Economies:

As the firm expands, it enjoys internal economies of production. It may be able to install better machines, sell its products more easily, borrow money cheaply, procure the services of more efficient manager and workers, etc. All these economies help in increasing the returns to scale more than proportionately.

iv) External Economies:

A firm also enjoys increasing returns to scale due to external economies. When the industry itself expands to meet the increased long-run demand for its product, external economies appear which are shared by all the firms in the industry. When a large number of firms are concentrated at one place, skilled labour, credit and transport facilities are easily available. Subsidiary industries crop up to help the main industry. Trade journals, research and training centres appear which help in increasing the productive efficiency of the firms. Thus these external economies are also the cause of increasing returns to scale.

2) Constant Returns to Scale :

Returns to scale become constant as the increase in total output is in exact proportion to the increase in inputs. If the scale of production is increased further, total returns will increase in such a way that the marginal returns become constant. In the table, for the 4th and 5th units of the scale of production, marginal returns are 11, i.e., returns to scale are constant. In the figure, the portion from C and D of the RS curve is horizontal which depicts constant returns to scale. It means that increments of each input are constant at all levels of output.

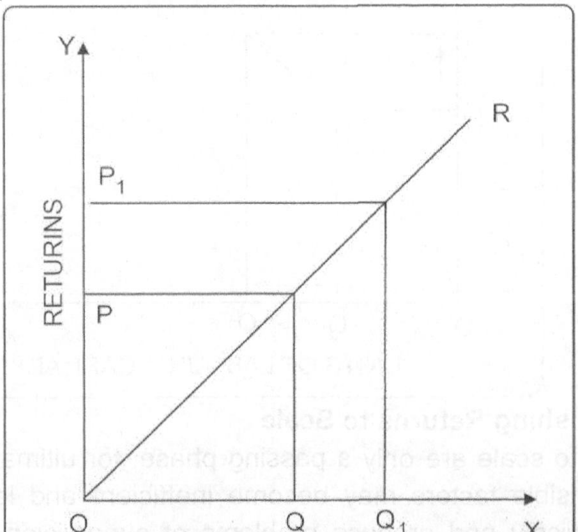

Causes of Constant Returns to Scale

Returns to scale are constant due to:

i) Internal Economies and Diseconomies :

But increasing returns to scale do not continue indefinitely. As the firm expands further, internal economies are counterbalance by internal diseconomies. Returns increase in the same proportion so that there are constant returns in scale over a large range of output.

ii) External Economies and Diseconomies :

The returns to scale are constant when external diseconomies and economies are neutralized and output increases in the same proportion.

iii) Divisible Factors :

When factors of production are perfectly divisible, substitutable, and homogeneous with perfectly elastic supplies at given prices, returns to scale are constant.

3) Diminishing Returns to Scale

Returns to scale diminish because the increase in output is less than proportional to the increase in inputs. The table shows that when output is increased from the 6th, 7th and 8th units, the total returns increase at a lower rate than before so that the marginal returns start diminishing successively to 10, 9 and 8. In the figure, the portion from D to S of the RS curve shows diminishing returns.

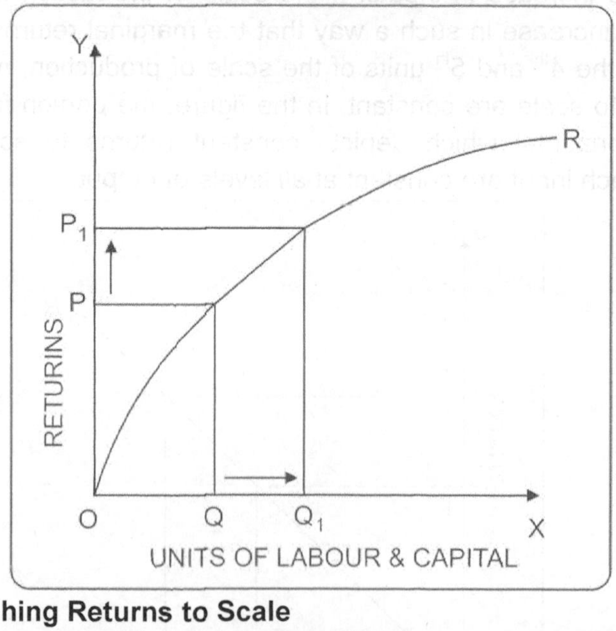

Causes of Diminishing Returns to Scale

Constant returns to scale are only a passing phase, for ultimately returns to scale start diminishing. Indivisible factors may become inefficient and less productive. Business may become unwisely and produce problems of supervision and coordination. Large management creates difficulties of control and rigidities. To these internal diseconomies are added external diseconomies of scale. These arise from higher factor prices or from diminishing productivities of the factors. As the industry continues to expand, the demand for skilled labour, land, capital, etc. rises. There being perfect competition, intensive bidding raises wages, rent and interest. Prices of raw materials also go up. Transport and marketing difficulties emerge. All these factors tend to raise costs and the expansion of the firm's leads to diminishing returns to scale so that doubling the scale would not lead to doubling the scale would not lead to doubling the output.

Conclusion

For the management increasing, decreasing or constant returns to scale reflect changes in production efficiency that result from scaling up productive inputs. But returns to scale is strictly a production and cost concept. Management's decision on what to produce and how much to produce must be based upon the demand for the product. Therefore, demand and other factors must also be considered in decision making.

4.5 Economies of Scale: Internal and External Economies :

A) REAL INTERNAL ECONOMIES :

Real internal economies are "associated with a reduction in the physical quantity of inputs, raw materials, various types of labour and various types of capital (fixed or circulating) used by a large firm". Real internal economies which arise from the expansion of a firm are the following:

1) Labor Economies :

As the firm expands, it achieves labor economies with increased division of labor and specialization. When a firm expands in size, this necessitates division of labor whereby each worker is assigned one particular job, and the splitting of processes into sub-processes for greater efficiency and productivity. This in turn, leads to produce goods, and to the invention of large number of labor-saving machines, according to Adam Smith. Thus division of labor and specialization lead to greater productive efficiency and reduction in per unit cost in a large firm.

2) Technical Economies :

Technical economies are associated with all types of machines and equipments used by a large firm. They arise from the use of better follows:

i) Economies of Indivisibility :

Mrs. Joan Robinson refers to economies of factor indivisibility. Fixed capital is one such factor. It is indivisible in sense that a machine, an equipment or a plant must be used in a fixed minimum size or capacity to justify its use. Such machines can be most efficiently used at a fairly large output than at small outputs because they cannot be divided into smaller units. For example, an automated car assembly plant is not a viable proposition, if the number of cars to be assembled is small because much of the plant would remain idle. But a large firm assembling a large number of cars may be able to utilize the plant to its full capacity and achieve lower per unit cost.

ii) Economies of Superior Technique :

It is only a large firm which can afford to pay for costly machines and install them. Such machines are more productive than small machines. The high cost of such machines can be spread over a larger output which they help to produce. Thus the per unit cost of production falls in a large firm which employs costly and superior plant and equipment and thereby enjoys a technical superiority over a small firm.

iii) Economies of Increased Dimensions :

The installation of large machines itself brings many advantages to a firm. The cost of operating large machines is less than that of operating small machines. Even the cost of construction is relatively lower for large machines than for small ones. The cost of manufacture of a double-decker carries more passengers than a single-decker and at the same time requires only a driver and a conductor like a latter. Thus its operating costs are relatively lower.

3) Marketing Economies :

A large firm also reaps the economies of buying and selling. It buys its requirements of various inputs in bulk and is, therefore, able to secure them at favorable terms in the form of better quality inputs, prompt delivery, transport concessions, etc. Because of its larger organization, it produces quality products which are offered for the sale in attractive packing by its packing department. It may also have a sales department manned by experts who carry on salesmanship, propaganda and advertisement through the various media efficiently. Thus a large firm is able to reap the economies of marketing through its superior bargaining power and efficient packing and sales organization.

4) Managerial Economies :

A large firm can afford to put specialists to supervise and manage the various departments. There may be a separate head for manufacturing, assembling, packing, marketing, general administration, etc. This decentralization leads to functional specialization which increases the productive efficiency of the firm. "Large firms apply techniques of management involving a high degree of mechanization, such as telephones, telex machines, television screen and computers. These techniques save time in decision making process and speed up the processing of information, as well as increasing its amount and its accuracy." These managerial economies also reduce per unit cost of management because with expansion of the firm, the various departmental managers will manage large output as efficiently as they were managing small output at the same salary.

5) Risk-Bearing Economies :

A large firm is in a better position than a small firm in spreading its risks. It can produce a variety of products, and sell them in different areas. By the diversification of its products the large firm is able to reduce risks by counter-balancing the loss of one product by the gain from other products. By the diversification of markets, it can counter-balance the fall in demand in one market by the increased demand in other markets. Even if the demand in the other markets for the products of the firm is constant, the loss can be easily borne by it.

6) Economies of Research :

A large firm possesses larger resources than a small firm and can establish its own research laboratory and employ trained research workers. When they invent new production techniques or processes, the latter become the property of the firm which utilizes them for increasing its output and reducing costs.

B) Pecuniary Internal Economies :

Pecuniary or monetary internal economies accrue to a large firm solely through reductions in the market prices of its inputs. They arise when (i) it purchases raw material in bulk at lower prices from its suppliers; (ii) it gets loans from banks and other financial institutions at low interest rates because it processes large assets and good reputation; (iii) it raises capital by floating shares at a premium and debentures at low interest rates in the capital market; (iv) it advertises at concessional rates on a large scale in different media; (v) it transports large quantities of its commodity at concessional transport rates. Thus pecuniary economies are "realized from paying lower prices for the factors used in the production and distribution of the product, due to bulk-buying by in the firm as its size increases."

C) Real External Economies :

According to Prof. Viner, real external economies accrue to a firm in an industry due to technological influences on its output which reduces its real cost of production. They represent benefits to firms in an industry through technological interdependence of firms. Real external economies arise when the industry is localised in a particular area, makes inventions and evolves specialisation in production processes. These external economies are discussed below.

1) Technical Economies :

Technical external economies arise from specialization. When an industry expands in size, firms start specializing in different processes and the industry benefits on the whole. For example, in the cotton textile industry some firms may specialize in manufacturing thread, others in printing, still others in dyeing, some in long cloth, some in dhotis, some in shirting, etc, As a result, the productive efficiency of the firms specializing in different fields increases and the unit cost of production falls.

Further, subsidiary industries develop to supply the localized industry with tools, equipment and raw materials, and special services for repairs and maintenance of plants and equipments, thereby lowering the unit cost of production of all the firms.

2) Economies of Information :

As an industry expands, it specializes in collecting and discriminating market information, in marketing the industry's product and in supplying the firms with consultant services. An industry is in a better position to set up research laboratories than a large firm because it is able to pool larger resources. It can employ highly paid and more experienced research personnel. The fruits of their research in the form of new of new inventions are passed on to the firms through a scientific journal. The industry can also set up an information centre which may publish a journal and pass on information regarding the availability of raw materials, modern machines, export potentialities of the products of the industry in various countries of the world and provide other information needed by the firms. All this helps in raising the productive efficiency of the firms and reduction in their costs.

3) Economies of By-products :

When an industry is localized, it turns large quantities of waste materials, such as molasses in sugar industry and iron scrap in steel industry. New firms enter the industry which purchase these waste materials at reasonable prices and use them for manufacturing by-products. The firms in the industry are able to reduce per unit cost in two ways: first, they do not incur expenses in disposing of the waste materials, and second, they earn some amount by selling them to manufacturers of by-products.

D) Pecuniary External Economies :

Pecuniary external economies arise to firm an industry from reductions in factor prices. They reflect an interdependence among firms which is transmitted through factor price reductions in the industry. Such reductions in factor prices may arise from a number of sources. (1) Local educational institutions may specialize in the type of courses needed by the industry, thereby making available skilled labor to all the firms. (2) Local management consultants can develop specialist expertise. (3) Firms with similar requirements can produce a pool of workers and managers with the required skills to meet the needs of the local labor market. (4) The transport and communications infrastructure can be developed to meet the special needs of the industry. The industry may ask the railways for additional facilities for more wagons, loading and unloading, etc. Road transporters may also provide special facilities to firms at concessional rates. (5) The Electricity Company or board may supply adequate and continuous power to the firms at concessional rates. (6) Banks, insurance companies and other financial institutions may open their offices in the area and provide cheap and timely credit and insurance facilities.

E) Relation between Internal and External Economies :

The relation between internal and external economies is only one of degree. For example, firms may be enjoying external economies, but if they combine together, then all external economies become internal for them. Again, an internal economy reaped by a firm becomes external to some other firm if it uses the same. To take an example, if molasses are used by the sugar factory itself for manufacturing spirit, it is an internal economy. But if some other firm buys a molasses for manufacturing spirit, it is external economy to the buying firm.

Often external economies lead to internal economies. As pointed out by Mrs. Robinson, "Economies of large scale industry are likely to have the effect of altering the optimum size of the firm, and the reorganization of the firm to adapt itself to the new optimum size may lead to further economies. These have been described by Prof. Robertson as internal-external economies. These have been demise, because they depend upon the size of the firm and external economies because they depend upon the size of the industry."

DISECONOMIES OF SCALE

A diseconomy of scale exits when larger output leads to higher per unit cost. The economies of scale cannot continue indefinitely. A time comes in the life of a firm or an industry when further expansion leads to diseconomies in place of economies. Internal and external diseconomies are, in fact, the limits to large scale productions. We discuss below real and pecuniary internal and external diseconomies.

A) Real Internal Diseconomies :

When a firm expands beyond an optimum level, a number of problems arise such as factor shortages, lack of coordination and management, marketing and technological difficulties, etc. They tend to rise per unit cost of production. Thus real internal diseconomies arise from the following:

1) Managerial Diseconomies :

The check to the further expansion of a firm is put due to the failure on the part of the management to supervise and control the business property. There is a limit beyond which a firm becomes unwieldy and hence unmanageable. Supervision becomes lax. Workers do not work efficiently, wastages arise, decision-making becomes difficult, coordination between workers and management disappears and per unit cost increases.

2) Marketing Diseconomies :

The expansion of a firm beyond a certain limit may also involve marketing problems. Raw materials may not be available in sufficient quantities due to their scarcities. The demand for the products of the firm may fall as a result of changes in tastes of the people and firm may not be in a position to change accordingly in the short period. The market organization may fail to foresee changes in market conditions whereby the sales might fall.

3) Technical Diseconomies :

A large scale firm often operates heavy capital equipment which is indivisible. As the firm expands its size beyond the optimum level, there are repeated breakdowns in plants and equipments and the firm may fail to operate its plant to its maximum capacity. It may have excess capacity or idle capacity. As a result, per unit cost increases.

4) **Diseconomies of Risk Taking :**

   As the scale of production of a firm expands, risks also increase with it. An error of judgment on the part of the sales manager or the production manager may adversely affect sales or production which may lead to a great loss.

B) **Pecuniary Internal Diseconomies :**

   Pecuniary internal diseconomies arise when the prices of factors used in the production and distribution of the commodity increase. As a firm expands, it may need more labor, raw materials, finance, etc. But trained and skilled labor may be available at higher wages. There may arise shortages of raw materials which it may have to buy at higher prices. More finance may be available at high interest rate. Marketing, sales and transport expenses may increase with the expansion of the firm. All these physical factors tend to rise per unit cost.

C) **Pecuniary External Diseconomies :**

   Pecuniary external diseconomies arise solely through increases in the market prices of inputs of an industry. As an industry expands, pecuniary external diseconomies arise when the prices of factors increase. When an industry expands, the demand for factors like labour, capital equipment, raw materials, etc. increases on the part of firms which may eventually raise their prices. But the localization of an industry and its overgrowth may lead to

4.6 Cost Analysis :

Cost analysis is all about the study of the behavior of cost e.g Total cost, Average cost, marginal cost etc. With respect to various production criteria like the scale of operations, prices of the factors of production, size of output, etc. It is all about the financial aspects of production. In order to understand the cost function well, in this chapter, we will look at various cost concepts.

A) **Definition of Cost Concept :**

a) **Meaning of cost :**

   Cost refers to payment made to the factor owner for using their servicing in production process.

   The term 'cost' is most widely used as the 'money cost' of production which relates to the money expenditure of a firm on:

a. wages and salary paid to labor

b. payment for rent

c. payment for raw material, power, fuel etc.

d. payment to government as taxes and fees.

e. Payment to machine and equipments.

b) **Classification of cost :**

   Explicit Cost is the cost which is actually incurred on external factors or which is not own by the organization, during production. On the other hand, **Implicit Cost**, are just opposite to the explicit cost, incurred on internal factors or own by firm. As the organization does not directly incur them, but they are implied in nature which does not involve a cash payment. The former is an out of pocket cost, while the latter is an opportunity cost.

c) The opportunity cost :

The opportunity cost to a firm in using any input is what the input could earn in its best alternative use (outside the firm). This is true for inputs purchased or hired by the firm as well as for inputs owned and used by the firm in its own production. For example, a firm must pay wages of $20,000 per year to one of its employees if that is the amount the worker would earn in his or her best alternative occupation in another firm. If this firm attempted to pay less, the worker would simply seek employment in the other firm. Similarly, if the entrepreneur could earn more in managing another firm than in directing his or her own firm, it would not make much economic sense to continue to be self-employed. Thus, for a firm to retain any input for its own use, it must include as a cost the opportunity cost that the input could earn in its best alternative use or employment. This is the **alternative** or **opportunity cost doctrine.** Similarly, the opportunity cost of attending college includes not only the explicit cost of tuition, books, and so on, but also the foregone earnings of not working

Costs are also classified into private and social.

Private costs are the opportunity costs incurred by *individuals and firms* in the process of producing goods and services. **Social costs** are the costs incurred by *society* as a whole. Social costs are higher than private costs when firms are able to escape some of the economic costs of production. For example, a firm dumping untreated waste into the air imposes a cost on society (in the form of higher cleaning bills, more breathing ailments, and so on) that is not reflected in the costs of the firm. Private costs can be made equal to society costs by public regulation requiring the firm to install antipollution equipment.

1) COST IN THE SHORT RUN :

In this section, we examine the theory of cost in the short run. We first decline fixed, variable, and total costs and draw these total cost curves. We then define average fixed cost, average variable cost, average total cost, and marginal cost and draw these per-unit cost curves. Finally, we show how per-unit cost curves can be derived graphically from the corresponding total cost curves.

TOTAL COSTS

In the short run, some inputs are fixed and some are variable; this leads to fixed and variable costs.

Total fixed costs:

Total fixed costs (TFC), are the total obligations of the firm per time period for all fixed inputs. These fixed or sunk costs include payments for renting the plant and equipment for the (or depreciation on plant and equipment if the firm owns them), most kinds of insurance, property taxes, and some salaries (such as those of top management, which are fixed by contract and must be paid over the life of the contract whether the firm produces or not). Fixed costs are sometimes referred to as *sunk costs* by economists and *overhead costs* by business people.

Total variable costs:

Total variable costs (TVC) are the total obligations of the firm per time period for all the variable inputs of the firm. These include payments for raw materials, fuels, most types of labor, excise taxes, and so on.

Total costs = TFC + TVC.

B) Behavior of cost curves (Short Run) :

Within the limits imposed by the given plant, the firm can vary its output in the short run by varying the quantity of the variable inputs used per period of time. This gives rise to TFC, TVC and TC schedules and curves. These show, respectively, the *minimum fixed,* variable, and total costs of producing the various levels of output in the short run. In defining these cost schedules and curves, all inputs are valued at their opportunity cost, which includes both explicit and implicit costs.

Table presents hypothetical TFC, TVC, and TC schedules. These schedules are then plotted in Figure. We see that TFC are $30 regardless of the level of output. This is reflected in Figure in the horizontal TFC curve at the level of $30, TVC are zero when output is zero and rise as output rises. The shape of the TVC curve follows directly from the law of diminishing returns. Up to the point of inflection, the firm uses so little of the variable inputs with the fixed inputs that the law of diminishing returns is not yet operating. As a result, the TVC curve faces downwards or rises at a decreasing rate. Past point W (i.e., for output levels greater than 1.5), the law of diminishing returns operates and the TVC curve faces upward or rises at an increasing rate. Since TC= TFC + TVC, the TC curve has the same shape as the TVC curve but is $30 (the TFC) above it at each output level.

TABLE Fixed, Variable, and Total Costs

Labor	Quantity	Fixed Cost	Variable Cost	Total Cost
1	16	$160	$80	$240
2	40	$160	$160	$320
3	60	$160	$240	$400

Labor	Quantity	Fixed Cost	Variable Cost	Total Cost
4	72	$160	$320	$480
5	80	$160	$400	$560
6	84	$160	$480	$640
7	82	$160	$560	$720

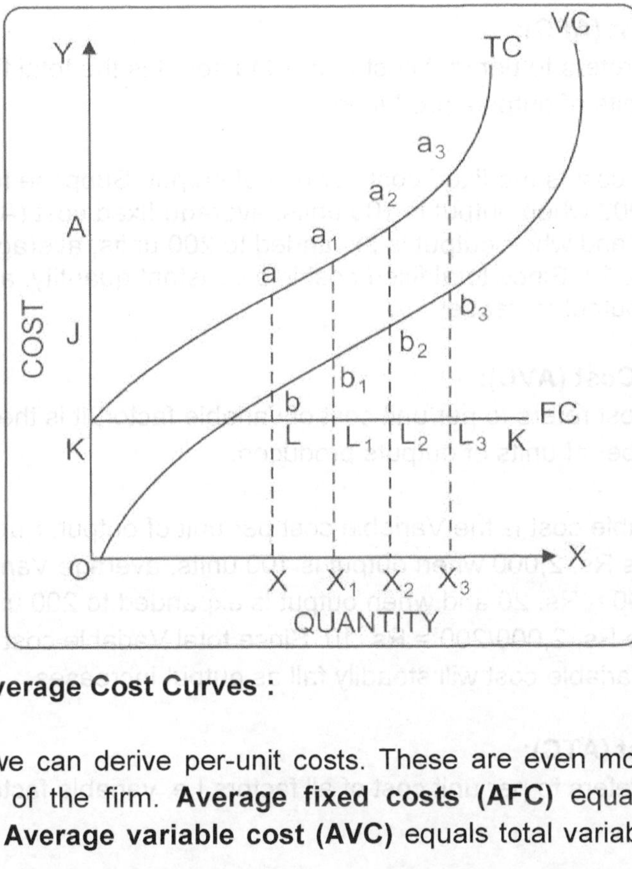

The Short-Run Average Cost Curves :

Per-Unit Costs

From total costs we can derive per-unit costs. These are even more important in the short-run analysis of the firm. **Average fixed costs (AFC)** equals total fixed costs divided by output. **Average variable cost (AVC)** equals total variable costs divided by output.

Labor	Quantity	Fixed Cost	Variable Cost	Total Cost	Marginal Cost	Average Total Cost	Average Variable Cost
1	16	160	$80	240	5.00	15.00	5.00
2	40	160	160	320	3.30	8.00	4.00
3	60	160	240	400	4.00	6.60	4.00

Labor	Quantity	Fixed Cost	Variable Cost	Total Cost	Marginal Cost	Average Total Cost	Average Variable Cost
4	72	160	320	480	6.60	6.60	4.40
5	80	160	400	560	10.00	7.00	5.00
6	84	160	480	640	20.00	7.60	5.70

Average Fixed Cost (AFC):

Average fixed cost refers to per unit cost of fixed factor, it is the total fixed cost divided by the number of units of outputs produced.

AFC = TFC/Q

Thus average fixed cost is the fixed cost per unit of output. Suppose for a firm the total fixed cost is Rs. 2,000 when output is 100 units, average fixed cost (AFC) will be Rs. 2,000/100 = Rs. 20 and when output is expanded to 200 units, average fixed cost will be Rs. 2,000/200 = Rs. 10. Since total fixed cost is a constant quantity, average fixed cost will steadily fall as output increases.

Average Variable Cost (AVC):

Average Variable cost refers to per unit cost of variable factor, it is the total variable cost divided by the number of units of outputs produced.

AVC = TVC/Q

Thus average Variable cost is the Variable cost per unit of output. Suppose for a firm the total Variable cost is Rs. 2,000 when output is 100 units, average Variable cost (AVC) will be Rs. 2,000/100 = Rs. 20 and when output is expanded to 200 units, average Variable cost will be Rs. 2,000/200 = Rs. 10. Since total Variable cost is a constant quantity, average Variable cost will steadily fall as output increases.

Average Total Cost (ATC):

Average total cost refers to per unit cost of all factors I.e. variable factors and Fixed factors.

ATC = TC/Q

Thus average Total cost is the Total cost per unit of output. Suppose for a firm the total Total cost is Rs. 2,000 when output is 100 units, average Total cost (AVC) will be Rs. 2,000/100 = Rs. 20 and when output is expanded to 200 units, average Total cost will be Rs. 2,000/200 = Rs. 10. Since total Total cost is a constant quantity, average Total cost will steadily fall as output increases.

ATC = TC/Q

OR

ATC = AFC + AVC

MARGINAL COST

DEFINITION OF MARGINAL COST

Marginal cost is one of the most important concepts in all of economics. **Marginal cost** (MC) denotes the extra or additional cost of producing 1 extra unit of output or we can say change in total cost due to production of one more unit is called Marginal cost. Say a firm is producing 1000 compact discs for a total cost of \$10,000, If the total cost of producing 1001 discs is \$10,006, then the marginal cost of production is \$6 for the 1001st disc.

MC = TCn – TCn-1

Sometimes, the marginal cost of producing an extra unit of output can be quite low. For an airline flying plane with empty seats, the added cost of another passenger is literally peanuts; no additional capital (planes) or labor (pilots and flight attendant) is necessary. In other cases, the marginal cost of another unit of output can be quite high. Consider an electric utility. Under normal circumstances, it can generate enough power using only its lowest-cost, most efficient plants. But on a hot summer day, when everyone's air conditioners are running and demand for electricity is high, the utility may be forced to turn on its old, high-cost, inefficient generators. This added electric power comes at a high marginal cost to the utility.

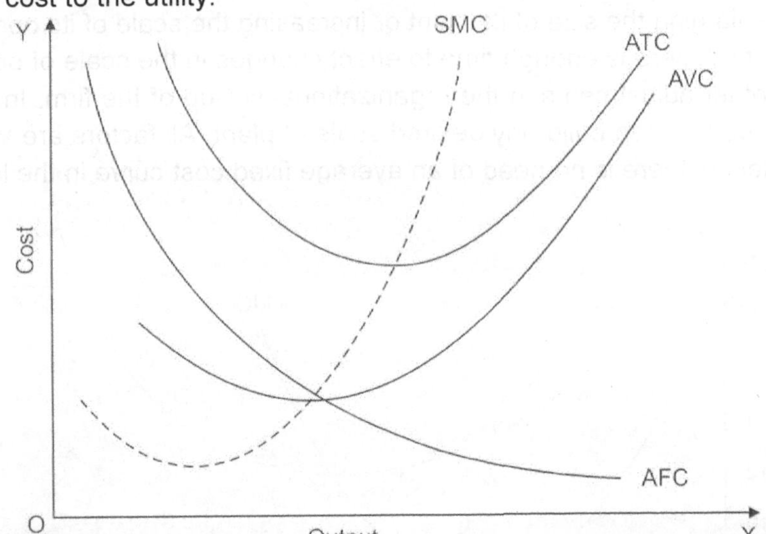

- **The relationship between average cost curve and marginal cost curve can be summed up as follows:**
  1. When marginal cost is less than the average cost, average cost falls with increase in output. It will be seen from fig. that as long as MC curve lies below the ATC curve (up to OQ2 amount of output), ATC curve slopes downwards. It does not matter whether the MC curve with AVC curve also.

2. When marginal cost is greater than the average cost, average cost is rising. In fig., MC curve lies above ATC curves beyond OQ2. Level of output and in this range, ATC curve is rising.
3. When marginal cost is equal to average cost, average cost is constant. In Fig. average cost is minimum and constant for a while at point L on ATC curve, and MC curve cuts the ATC curve at this minimum point showing that marginal cost equals average cost.

➢ **WHY THE SHORT-RUN AVERAGE IS COST CURVE 'U-SHAPED'?**

In the short-run period, the average total cost (ATC) curve is U -shaped because of **the law of variable proportions.** This states that as more and more units of a **variable factor** are applied with **fixed factor, initially, the total product increases but would decreases eventually. Therefore, initially cost is less and eventually it is more. Generally, price and output has inverse relationship.**

2) LONG-RUN COST CURVES :

We will now consider the shape of the long-period cost curves. Earlier, we have seen that in the short period the firm does not have adequate time to change the size of its plant or the scale of its operations. But in the long period there is no such difficulty. If the demand for the firm's product increases, the firm can increase its output by enlarging the size of its plant or increasing the scale of its operations. So in the long period there is enough time to effect changes in the scale of operations or to introduce other adjustments in the organizational set-up of the firm. In fact, the firm, in the long period, can build any desired scale of plant. All factors are **variable,** none is **fixed.** Hence, there is no need of an average fixed cost curve in the long period.

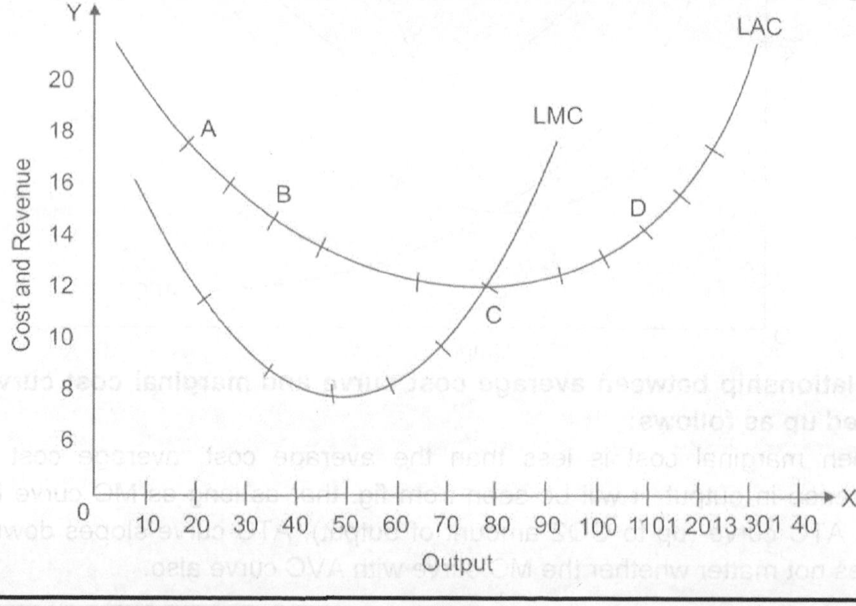

It can be generalized that the long-run cost curves are also, like shot-run cost curves, U-shaped. The only difference is that the long-run cost curves are flatter than the short-run cost curves, or the U-shape of the long-run cost curves is less pronounced than that of the short-run cost curves. In other words, the U-shape of a cost curve will be less pronounced, the longer the period to which the curve relates. Now the question is; Why is the U-shape of a long-run cost curve ?

less pronounced than that of a short-run cost curve? We can answer this question both at the simple as well as at the advanced level. The simple explanation of this trend is to be found in the behavior of the fixed and variable costs. It should be remembered that the fixed costs do not have the same importance in the long as in the short period. In the long period, there is adequate time available to change even the fixed factors. The fixed factors, in fact, become variable factors in the long period. Few factors remain fixed in the long period. If the demand for the product decreases in the long period and the firm reduces its output in response to the diminished demand, it will do so not only by reducing the variable but also the fixed factors. For example, the firm may let out the unwanted building to others; it may reduce its administrative and marketing staff; it may also cut down its insurance premium. Consequently, the total fixed cost can be cut down to a considerable extent over a long period, whereas in the short period, fixed cost is 'fixed' absolutely. Likewise, if the demand for the product of the firm goes up in the long period, the firm can increase its output not only by increasing the variable but also the fixed factors. For example, it can acquire additional premises; it can increase the administrative and marketing staff; it can go in for additional insurance policies. In this manner, the fixed costs can vary to a considerable extent over long periods of time.

Points to be remember

4.1 Meaning of Supply

"A certain Quantity of Commodity which the producer is willing to sell at a particular price and particular period of time."

LAW OF SUPPLY:

The law of supply states that, other things remaining the same. ,the quantity of any commodity that firms

4.2 Production function

Production function (showing the input combinations that the firm can use to produce various levels of output) and the price of inputs, we can derive the firm's cost functions.

Q = f (L, C, N)

4.3 law of variable proportion

"As the proportion of the factor in a combination of factors is increased after a point, first the marginal and then the average product of that factor will diminish." Benham

Statement of Law

"The law of variable proportion states that more and more variables increases with given amount of fixed factors, total output will increase, but beyond some point the resulting output increases will become smaller and smaller."

Total production

Amount of production produced by producer after using all the factors e.g. variables factors and fixed factors in given time period

Average production

Output of per unit variable factor is called average production.

Average production = TP /L

4.4 Marginal Production

Amount of production derived from every additional unit of variable factor is called marginal production.

Marginal production = $TP_n - TP_{n-1}$

4.5 THE LAW OF RETURNS TO SCALE

The law of returns to scale describes the relationship between outputs and scale of inputs in the long-run when all the inputs are increased in the same proportion.

4.6 ECONOMIES OF SCALE: INTERNAL AND EXTERNAL ECONOMIES

A) REAL INTERNAL ECONOMIES :

i) Labour Economies.

ii) Technical Economies :

Technical economies are associated with all types of machines and equipments used by a large firm. They arise from the use of better follows:

a) Economies of Indivisibility.

b) Economies of Superior Technique

iii) Economies of Increased Dimensions

iv) Marketing Economies :

Concessions, etc. Because of its larger organization, it produces quality products which are offered for the sale in attractive packing by its packing department

v) Managerial Economies.

vi) Risk-Bearing Economies-

B) Economies of Research Pecuniary Internal Economies :

C) Real External Economies :

a) Technical Economies.

b) Economies of Information.

D) Economies of By-products.

E) Pecuniary External Economies

F) Relation between Internal and External Economies.

DISECONOMIES OF SCALE

A diseconomy of scale exits when larger output leads to higher per unit cost. The economies of scale cannot continue indefinitely.

Real Internal Diseconomies

1) **Managerial Diseconomies..**
2) **Marketing Diseconomies**
3) **Technical Diseconomies.**
4) **Diseconomies of Risk Taking.** As the scale of production of a firm expands, risks also increase with it. An error of judgement on the part of the sales manager or the production manager may adversely affect sales or production which may lead to a great loss.

A) Pecuniary Internal Diseconomies

B) Pecuniary External Diseconomies

Meaning of cost

Cost refers to payment made to the factor owner for using their servicing in production process.

Classification of cost

Explicit Cost is the cost which is actually incurred on external factors or which is not own by the organization, during production. On the other hand,

Implicit Cost, are just opposite to the explicit cost, incurred on internal factors or own by firm

The opportunity cost

The opportunity cost to a firm in using any input is what the input could earn in its best alternative use (outside the firm).

Private costs are the opportunity costs incurred by *individuals and firms* in the process of producing goods and services.

Social costs are the costs incurred by *society* as a whole.

COST IN THE SHORT RUN :

In this section, we examine the theory of cost in the short run. We first decline fixed, variable, and total costs and draw these total cost curves.

TOTAL COSTS :

In the short run, some inputs are fixed and some are variable; this leads to fixed and variable costs.

Total fixed costs:

Total fixed costs (TFC), are the total obligations of the firm per time period for all fixed inputs.

Total variable costs:

are the total obligations of the firm per time period for all the variable inputs of the firm.

Total costs = TFC + TVC.

Per-Unit Costs :

From total costs we can derive per-unit costs. These are even more important in the short-run analysis of the firm. **Average fixed costs (AFC)** equals total fixed costs divided by output. **Average variable cost (AVC)** equals total variable costs divided by output.

Average Fixed Cost (AFC):

Average fixed cost refers to per unit cost of fixed factor, it is the total fixed cost divided by the number of units of outputs produced.

AFC = TFC/Q

Average Variable Cost (AVC):

Average Variable cost refers to per unit cost of variable factor, it is the total variable cost divided by the number of units of outputs produced.

AVC = TVC/Q

Average Total Cost (ATC):

Average total cost refers to per unit cost of all factors I.e. variable factors and fixed factors.

ATC = TC/Q

or

ATC = AFC + AVC

MARGINAL COST :

Marginal cost (MC) denotes the extra or additional cost of producing 1 extra unit of output or we can say change in total cost due to production of one more unit is called marginal cost

MC = TCn – TCn-1

WHY THE SHORT-RUN AVERAGE IS COST CURVE 'U-SHAPED'?

In the short-run period, the average total cost (ATC) curve is U -shaped because of **the law of variable proportions.**

Questions for discussion

➢ **Write the answers in details of following question.**

1) What is law of supply?
2) What is production function?
3) Explain law of variable proportion?
4) Explain returns to scale?
5) What are the economies and diseconomies and how it effect in long run cost curve?
6) What is cost of production? What are the types of cost of production?
7) Write the relation between TFC, TVC and TC in short run
8) What is marginal cost?
9) Write relation between average and marginal cost curve behavior in short run.
10) Why the long run average total cost curve is 'U' shaped?

ꕥ Notes ꕥ